To Bro. John Everett,

Enjoy reading my

journeys.

Thomas Osborne

FROM THE PROJECTS TO THE PEACE CORPS TO THE PROFESSORIATE

A TRAVELING MEMOIR

DR. THOMAS O. EDWARDS

authorHOUSE®

AuthorHouse™
1663 Liberty Drive
Bloomington, IN 47403
www.authorhouse.com
Phone: 1 (800) 839-8640

Published by AuthorHouse   07/17/2017

ISBN: 978-1-5246-9878-2 (sc)
ISBN: 978-1-5246-9879-9 (hc)
ISBN: 978-1-5246-9877-5 (e)

Library of Congress Control Number: 2017910507

Print information available on the last page.

CONTENTS

INTRODUCTION

When one is born into the world, he/she becomes a part of the vast universe and automatically is inducted into the human race, which is composed of countless individuals. The person's immediate environment is an infinitesimal microcosm of all that exists in the expansive world. An individual's lifetime does not permit him/her to experience or comprehend the totality of the cosmos. Through travel, however, one can acquire a glimpse of the varied sceneries, cultures, and peoples that populate the universe. Travel expands the individual's personal knowledge in so many aspects: one develops an intense appreciation of the physical environment in other localities; one acknowledges the ingenuity of other individuals as they negotiate myriad challenges in their respective milieu; and one emphatically embraces his/her humanity vis-à-vis interactions with other individuals whose realities are radically different. As can be determined from the above, travels offer many enhancements for those who can experience these life-changing adventures.

Others, however, who may not choose to travel extensively, can experience travels vicariously and thereby enrich their emotional and cognitive capacities. A plethora of books have been written about travel, both fiction and nonfiction. Just think for a moment about classics such as *Gulliver's Travels* by Jonathan Swift and *Robinson Crusoe* by Daniel Defoe. Reading these works, one gains insights into how other people live, even if from an imaginary perspective, and the reader can enjoy the characters' experiences in distant lands.

In *From the Projects to the Peace Corps to the Professoriate*, I do not attempt to compare this work with the genius of the above canonical works. Nevertheless, this book does chronicle my diverse travels and provides nuances of these experiences throughout the memoir. Some vicarious learning about nonfictional travel also can be attained.

Another aspect of this book evokes Booker T. Washington's *Up from Slavery*. Whereas Washington's autobiography delineates how he began from a meager beginning and later achieved national and international renown, I also emanated from substandard means, yet achieved admirable success in the academic and professional arena.

This memoir begins with my childhood and teen years and traces my professional life through a long tenure in academia. Traveling experiences serve as the core of the work. Interwoven into the travels is my participation in humanitarian, academic, and professional endeavors. Several projects involved attempting to improve others' lives in foreign countries by assisting in the construction of churches, schools, and health care facilities. Other international travels related to the supervision of students who traveled abroad for field experience to enhance their academic pursuits. Highlighted in this work are my academic and professional presentations of empirical research and theoretical discourse at international conferences. Some personal aspects of travel also are included, climaxing in my enstoolment as a tribal chief in Ghana, West Africa.

In sum, there is so much to enjoy and learn by taking this journey and engaging in this traveling memoir. Bon voyage!

CHAPTER 1

EARLY PROJECT DAYS

As a young boy growing up in New Bern, North Carolina, I remember when we moved from a house in Brown's Alley to the A-Building in Craven Terrace, the segregated projects in the Negro (we were not called black then) neighborhood. I was around eight years old, and my parents were separated at the time. My father lived in the same town, so I did see him occasionally, if only for brief moments. Most of my time was spent with my siblings; there were ten of us, with eight still residing at home and the two older sisters already married.

At that time project life was relatively safe, and our existence was like other families who had many children, such as the Bells, the Dixons, the Saunders, and the Suggs. We may have been poor, but I don't remember going without food or other basic necessities. Whatever was placed on the table, I ate. I thought it was normal to have biscuits (my mother made the best), molasses, and fat back for dinner. Often a plate of navy beans or rice with chicken feet did the honors.

In Craven Terrace, playing various games with the neighborhood children occupied my time when there was no school. We would play Hop and Skip, shoot marbles, and throw balls. When it was school time, however, we took it seriously and performed all of our assigned tasks. Chores at home were completed as scheduled, or we faced the consequences, usually corporal punishment. When I was around ten years old, I followed the older boys and went to caddy at the local golf course. I was able to get away with this because I was big for my age. Nevertheless, I encountered an even greater predicament. My mother would not have approved on my going to caddy if she had known about it. So I concealed my deceit by giving my mother thirty-cents of the $1.30 that I earned and telling her I got this money by cutting white people's grass. I didn't know what to do with the dollar, so I hid it between my mattress and box spring. In late summer, as my mother was cleaning my room and flipped the mattress, she found nine dollars wrapped in a handkerchief. She wanted to know where this money had come from; therefore, I had to confess that I had been caddying. My mother was not as angry as I thought she would be but instead was somewhat gratified. She used the money to buy my school clothes for the coming year. I felt somewhat proud of myself.

Another specific incident that I recall during my early project days was a bully who always used to beat me up. He was one of the neighborhood boys, and I was simply afraid to fight him, even though I was bigger in size. I guess it was my family's teaching not to engage in physical altercations that contributed to my timidity. It seemed that practically every other day this boy would beat me down. It was shameful to be treated this way and not respond. One day, however, I got tired of being picked on and beat up, so I fought him and gave him a good licking. Spectators were telling me to get him for beating me on Roundtree Street, on Cedar Street, on Miller Street, in front of the school, and so on. I responded and gave him everything I had. When the fight was over and I was going home, he followed me, yelling and swearing. I was afraid that my mother was going to punish me for fighting when she heard all the commotion, but she simply said, "You must have given him a good whupping." He never started another fight with me.

Later, we moved to the R-Building in the same Craven Terrace projects, as our family size changed; another sister got married. I was a preteen then. One vivid incident that I remember was one evening when a group of young boys around my age was playing football, with older boys coaching them. They were at the community center playground near my house. I was not permitted to be out late at night, but I sneaked out of the house so I could play with the others. When it was my turn to play quarterback, I stood over the center and said, "Do, do, do, do the ball." As you can surmise, I had a stuttering problem at the time. The older boys thought my speech issue was hilarious, and as a result this incident earned me the moniker Duball, which was more popular for me than my given name, Thomas Edwards. Some would ask, "Do you know Thomas Edwards?" and the answer would be no. But when they said, "You know—Duball," then the answer would be a resounding, "Of course! What about him?"

When I was fifteen, my mother died on April 2, 1958, shortly before her fortieth birthday. I recall that I was at my church, Mount Calvary Missionary Baptist, attending the revival service with my best friend, Bill Sykes, when the pastor announced that Rev. Leander Edwards' sister had passed. We immediately jumped up and ran to my aunt Annie Mae's house. When I saw her, even though she was crying, I concluded that there was a mistake because she was still alive. Then it occurred to me that it must be my mother who had died (She also was a sister of Rev. Edwards.), so we ran from one end of the projects to the other. And sure enough, my mother had gone home to glory.

After my mother's passing, my father took custody of all of us, and we moved to the H-Building in the same projects. During the summer of the same year, my brother, Gene, moved to Brooklyn, New York, and I joined him a month later. We lived with our maternal uncle Earl and his young family in the Fort Greene projects. We enrolled at the old Boys High School and traveled from Fort Greene to Bedford-Stuyvesant. Life in the Fort was a little more difficult because there were the Chaplains, a gang that tried to recruit me. I refused because my focus was on academic achievement and taking advantage of opportunities in New York, which were more plentiful than in New Bern. Otherwise, project life was filled with playing basketball and other sports. I managed to get involved in the Church of the Open Door, which was located adjacent to the Farragut Projects. The young people I associated with there were positive, but we had our fun, just as other adolescents did. I met my high school "love," who was from Farragut, and we shared our dreams with each other—she, becoming a pediatrician, and I, a lawyer. The youth activities at the church were a source of religious and social fulfillment.

DOMINICAN REPUBLIC (MINI-PEACE CORPS)

I was still living in Fort Greene Projects when I began my studies at City College of New York, and I also still was involved at the Church of the Open Door. A major undertaking occurred at the Church of the Open Door that catapulted me into developing and maintaining a passion for traveling. A young associate minister of the church, Andre Diaz, from the Dominican Republic (DR) organized a group of us young people to travel to the DR to assist in building a local church. We conducted all kinds of fund-raising activities to secure the funds to travel and fulfill the project. This was during the summer of my junior year at City College. Ten of us, including my brother Gene, participated in this missionary endeavor, and it became a life-changing experience for me.

We lived in a small town, San Pedro de Macoris, and were assigned to various families who treated us very well and assisted in every way possible. After the tasks of assisting in the physical construction of the church, we engaged in social activities with the local residents. We played basketball and baseball; went to the beach, Boca Chica, where I saw clear blue water for the first time; and mutually taught each other our respective languages. What an exciting and thrilling experience!

When we returned to the United States, my mind was made up: I would join the Peace Corps and return to the Dominican Republic.

Therefore, during my senior year at City College, I was occupied with applying for the Peace Corps and selecting DR as my first choice. I did get an acceptance letter from the Peace Corps—with an assignment to Costa Rica. My initial reaction was, "Where in the world is that?" I decided to accept the assignment, however, because I felt that I needed to leave the country during this time of racial consciousness development and radical opposition to the Vietnam War.

Construction of church in Dominican Republic

CHAPTER 2

PEACE CORPS VOLUNTEER TO COSTA RICA

TRAINING FOR PEACE CORPS ASSIGNMENT

Leaving Fort Greene Projects in the summer of 1965, I was extremely excited to venture off to volunteer for the Peace Corps. Initial training for the community development assignment occurred in San Marcos, Texas, at Southwest Texas State College; it consisted primarily of learning the culture and customs of Costa Rica, as well as studying Spanish intensively. Some instructors were native Costa Ricans (Ticos), while others were of various Latino backgrounds. We volunteers from all parts of the country, including Hawaii, began to intermingle and form a cohesive unit. When we had free time, we would sometimes go to a bar for beer or other refreshments. I recall our visiting a particular locale, and we were told that everyone could be served except me because I was a Negro (black). Even though all my friends were thirsty from the long journey to find the spot, they refused to accept service. I appreciated this camaraderie and solidarity, and it gave me greater respect and admiration for my fellow volunteers.

After our eight weeks in Texas, we were sent to Arecibo, Puerto Rico to continue our training. We were individually assigned to families who lived in remote areas. Since we would be community developers in Costa Rica, it was necessary for us to experience living in isolated, rural settings, where we would have to communicate in Spanish and survive without our accustomed amenities. I lived with a young man and his family. He and I would awake early in the morning, walk more than half a mile to his farm, and cultivate the land. At around ten in the morning, we would walk back to the house and have breakfast, which consisted of hot coffee (made mostly with hot milk and a little coffee) and bread. Then we would return to work the land, cutting weeds with a machete and plowing with the same tool. At around two o'clock we would come in for lunch, which consisted of rice and beans, sometimes meat, plantains, and yucca. After a couple of hours of rest (siesta), we made our final trip back to the farm and would work until sunset. Before bed we would have a very light supper, usually soup and bread. This experience was to indicate to us volunteers if we were really serious about the assignment of community development.

I am having coffee with other volunteers.

ASSIGNMENT IN COSTA RICA

Upon completion of the field training, we were ready for our travel to Costa Rica and to begin our individual assignments to various rural areas. I, however, was asked to accept an assignment at the University of Costa Rica in San Jose, the capital, as an assistant physical education instructor. The current Peace Corps volunteer at the university was completing his tour, and since I excelled in sports, the Peace Corps staff decided I was the ideal person for the replacement.

In San Jose, I lived with a middle-class family that had a wonderful house and all the modern conveniences. San Jose was a beautiful cosmopolitan city. At the university, my task was to assist in the men's physical education classes that met Monday through Thursday, 8:00–10:00 a.m. and 4:00–6:00 p.m., every other week. Therefore, I had an abundance of free time: one week with no classes, and during the week with classes, the hours between ten in the morning and four in the afternoon were without a schedule. To occupy all of that time, I decided to enroll in courses at the university, which were taught in Spanish, of course. I selected a beginning French course and a sociology class. Can you imagine my studying French in a Spanish-speaking university? I do recall that there was a particular phrase in French that the professor wanted the class to pronounce. It was difficult for the Spanish speaking students, but I was complimented on my ability to do it.

After the first semester of this arrangement, I felt very unfulfilled, dissatisfied, and despondent. I was living as well or even better than I'd lived in the projects back home, but the idealism that compelled me to join the Peace Corps was not being realized. Consequently, I requested a reassignment to a rural community, so that I could practice community development for which I was trained and simultaneously feel that I was assisting in improving the lives of others. As a Peace Corps volunteer, I simply was not comfortable pursuing a middle-class lifestyle in a modern city. It seemed like a great paradox. My request was granted, and I was assigned to a rural community in a remote area, Puerto Viejo de Sarapiqui. I was delighted because now I would no longer have the guilt of living in a metropolitan area with all the amenities.

When I arrived in Puerto Viejo, I started at once to put into practice my training as a community developer. I must mention that this locale had experience with other American volunteers, Mennonites, who were conscientious objectors in the States and had been serving in the community for several years. The Costa Ricans didn't understand initially how I was different from the Mennonites, but when they noticed that I would frequent bars and socialize by drinking and dancing, they realized that my mission there was quite different. I lived with a family for a few months until I was able to rent my own house. To many Ticos, this was strange because I didn't have a woman living with me. They constantly tried to marry me off with one of the local girls, who, incidentally, were gorgeous, but matrimony was not one of my objectives.

Thomas on horseback along with other volunteers.

INVESTIGATION METHODS IN PUERTO VIEJO DE SARAPIQUI

In Puerto Viejo, I began to assess the community by ascertaining what the people viewed as concerns. During the first month, I started a house-to-house campaign to introduce myself, as well as to gain insight into what the problems of the community were. I later found that this method did not prove successful; perhaps I hadn't considered the circumstances of the visits. Usually, I arrived during the day when the señor of the house was out working. The females of the house were always reluctant to talk about the community. They would answer *sí* or *no* politely but would not offer any information due to a lack of knowledge or maybe timidity. After visiting a few homes during the evening, usually after dark, and finding it difficult to communicate because the family might be having dinner or preparing to retire for the evening, I decided to abandon this method. Although, as mentioned, it was unsuccessful, I did learn of the attitudes of the people toward their community.

I later began to investigate more informally by talking to the *pulperia* (grocery store) owners and the people who were in the pulperia during various hours of the day. I went to the *cantinas* (bars) in the evening to intermingle and investigate. This method was useful, to a limited extent. The problem was that I very seldom encountered leaders or potential leaders at the cantinas and pool halls. The most successful method of investigating was obtaining the names of the members of the various committees, such as the school board and the Parent-Teacher Association, and talking with these individuals directly about the problems of the community. After investigating, I embarked upon a process of educating Puerto Viejo about the Peace Corps (*Cuerpo de Paz*) and its objectives.

EDUCATIONAL PROCESS

I participated in meetings called by the *patronato escolar* (school board) and other organizations. Originally, I used these opportunities to introduce myself and to explain the Cuerpo de Paz. I tried to explain community development (*desarrollo de le comunidad*) in general. However, even though my Spanish was more or less adequate and the meetings were well organized, these types of meetings were not as successful as I expected. Invariably, only a few people attended the meetings, mostly señoras. In conjunction with these meetings, I also presented films and used the opportunity to explain more about community development and the Peace Corps. Usually, when I presented films, the majority of the attendees were children—most people thought of films as entertainment for youngsters. On several occasions, I used printed materials, such as posters, to announce meetings. I would invite the entire town to the function, whether it was a meeting or presentation of films. However, only a few people would arrive. I also used personal written invitations. People were more responsive, but I could never get more than 10–15 percent of the adult population to attend these functions.

In evaluating my methods of educating the community, it appears they were inadequate because the events didn't attract the majority of the adults. The women stayed at home. The men stayed at home during the week, and on Saturdays and Sundays they spent the day entertaining themselves at the bars and pool halls. A television in one of the pulperias contributed to my unsuccessful attempt to educate the people about the Peace Corps, in general, and community development, specifically. Nevertheless, I participated in several ongoing projects, as well as initiating projects.

ONGOING PROJECTS

o   Bases for Cement Latrines

One project that was underway upon my arrival was the construction of bases for cement latrines, under the auspices of the Comité Bienestar Comunal (Committee for the Well-Being of the Community). The cement seats had been bought from the Ministry of Health. When the bases were completed, the entire sanitary structure would be sold to the people. I was asked to make the bases, along with the Mennonites. I agreed originally but refused later because only we three Americans were working, while the community was not involved. I tried to stimulate the community residents to assist with the endeavor, but after their refusal, I encouraged the Mennonites not to work if the committee would not help. I also emphasized the mission of the Peace Corps to the committee and the Mennonites. The chair of the committee called a meeting to discuss the situation. The Mennonites told the committee that they would only work if other members of the committee helped. The bases were made, and all the latrines were sold. The project was successful in terms of getting the job done, but from a community development perspective, it was not; there was practically no community involvement.

o   Health Concerns

Another project in progress was to secure a doctor for the area from the unidad móvil (mobile health unit). Since this was a matter for the Ministry of Health, I participated in the writing of letters and making continuous visits to the Ministry. After several months, we were successful in having a doctor sent to the area.

The construction of a community health center had been in progress for years in Puerto Viejo. The lots had been secured, as well as other building materials, such as blocks, sand, and some lumber. However, there had been no progress because no one in the town could assume the responsibility of directing the construction. The community residents were waiting for the Ministry of Health to send the foreman. Although the Committee for the Well-Being of the Community was never successful in obtaining personnel from the Ministry of Health, workers were sent from the Ministry of Transportation section for community development. The work progressed tremendously. In this project, community development was realized in many ways. The committee took responsibility for the task. It had several fund-raising activities to secure money in order to maintain the impetus and enthusiasm that existed when the work was initiated. The committee also employed three workers. In addition to paying the salaries for these three employees, it paid extra hours to the foreman and other workers from the Ministry of Health. Although volunteer workers did not arrive at the construction site as often as desired, from a community development perspective, the community cooperated in other forms. The people bought raffle tickets and attended committee functions. There also was confidence in the committee. The saying *"Hay que cooperar"* (Everyone must cooperate) was frequently uttered. In other words, the committee identified with the work and was proud of the progress. Several committee members said, when we completed this project, "Let's continue with the *caneria* [potable water supply] or the church." I purposely did not introduce other projects when this work was initiated. I realized that a lot of community development could be accomplished in this project. I tried to get the committee to keep the town informed of the progress so that the people would feel more identified with the work, and the committee did so on several occasions. The committee really did a commendable job overall. The members always talked about the construction. Some were more enthusiastic than others, even conducting activities on behalf of the committee without prior approval. In sum, the committee did a magnificent job with this project, but the community itself did not identify sufficiently with the work. Since this was the first project that the community had undertaken on a self-reliance basis, these problems were not beyond the ordinary.

INITIATED PROJECTS

o   Literacy Class

One of my first projects was starting a literacy class. During the investigation phase, several residents asked me if I would teach them to read and write. Two brothers, who were owners of a pulperia, were the most enthusiastic for the literacy class. The local teachers also gave me information and the names of others who were interested in this class. I obtained the materials from Alfalit, a literacy organization. The pulperia owners offered their salon for the classroom, but when all was prepared, no one came to the first or second class session. The most I did was to teach arithmetic to one person who already knew how to read and write. It was unfortunate that this program could not have been more successful because there were many individuals who could have benefited from it.

When the literacy class began, I also initiated an English class for the children of the community. The children attended this class after school and during the early afternoon when school was not in session. To my surprise, this endeavor was extremely fruitful; the children attended faithfully and were always eager to learn. They responded well to my teaching, and I enjoyed seeing them learn and flourish. I had never considered teaching as a career or as a noble profession, yet I realized that this involvement brought fulfillment to all parties involved. Unwittingly, I began my tenure as a professional educator.

o   Regional Association

I was told that Sarapiquì had a regional association when I arrived in Puerto Viejo. I immediately discovered that the regional association, if it existed, was inactive. I thought that trying to interest the people of the zone in having Sarapiquì cantonized would stimulate their desire to unite into a regional association. The idea of obtaining a *colegio* (high school) was also introduced with this project. Data were collected concerning the various populations of the region. Upon trying to explain the reasons for the regional association—such as changing the zone into a canton—I concluded that insoluble problems existed. For example, while talking about a regional association for the canton, the association was not of any importance. Where the seat of the canton was to be became the dominant issue of the conversation. Each town wanted the seat.

After a community development seminar in a neighboring town, Cuidad Quesada, the participants from my town were very interested in forming a regional association. We organized a general meeting for the purpose of informing the town of the topics discussed at the seminar and simultaneously creating a committee pro-canton Sarapiqui. The *regidores* (representatives) of the zone were invited to the meeting. Even though the purpose of the meeting was to form a regional association, no one from the other towns was invited. The organizers were aware of this fact. The scheme was to initiate in Puerto Viejo, to get ahead, and to make certain that Puerto Viejo would be the *cabezera* (seat) of the canton. After the project was well advanced, other towns would be invited to participate. However, since the regidores did not attend the meeting, the committee was not formed. I was very satisfied with this project because I had tried previously to interest the people into making Sarapiqui a canton. The only prior support that I could get was that the *diputados* had presented this idea to the General Assembly several times without concrete results. The initiatives of these individuals made me very content. They were trying to form a regional association and to create a committee pro-canton Sarapiqui.

In terms of the immediate perspectives of community development, I think that this project was a relatively successful one. The leading persons did educate the town by informing it of the regional seminar. The fact that the initiative originated from several individuals rather than from me signified success from both the immediate and the long-range perspectives of community development. Several of these individuals experienced their first opportunity to speak in public. It was lamentable that other towns were not invited to the meeting, as its purpose had regional implications. I realized from my participation with these persons that the endeavor for a regional association was futile unless there was mass education and mutual exigencies. Each town prided itself on possessing something that the other towns did not have; in other words, its uniqueness. This rivalry stimulated community action because each town wanted to be the most developed. Personally,

I felt that this competition was productive, but it should not impede regional action and cooperation.

o   4-S Club (Equivalent to 4-H Club in the USA)

After my arrival in Puerto Viejo, I decided to start a 4-S Club project. I spoke with the former extension agent concerning assisting me in the formation of the club, and he agreed to cooperate. We decided to look for leaders first. I found one young man who was well respected and appeared to be the ideal leader. He agreed to be the leader after he was acquainted with the organization. We gave him material to read to familiarize him with the national 4-S organization and its goals. However, during this time I discovered that he was not as interested as he had appeared initially. After several months, he still had not read the materials, so he returned them to me. Meanwhile, the extension agent and I decided to incorporate the 4-S into the entire zone, beginning in the neighboring town, La Virgin, and Puerto Viejo. It seemed that every time we followed our scheduled visit to La Virgin, the extension agent suddenly became occupied. After four or five times of excuses, I decided not to bother him further and decided to begin the 4-S Club myself in Puerto Viejo.

I had planned to organize the boys, and, subsequently, they would select their own leader. I realized that the 4-S meant nothing to the boys. The first job was to educate and interest them in the 4-S program. My tactic was to use the juvenile soccer team, Estrella Roja (Red Star). At this time, the team was poorly organized, so we decided to reorganize the team while simultaneously forming the 4-S Club. We had our first meeting to begin the reorganization and to introduce the 4-S Club. Obviously, the boys showed more interest when we discussed the soccer team. I decided to present information on the 4-S organization initially. Bulletins (*folletos*) were distributed, and each boy was asked to participate by reading a paragraph of the material. Some boys refused to read. While others were reading, the boys who refused to read would laugh and disturb the readers.

I was quite disappointed with the outcome of the meeting. I decided that it was better to concentrate on the organization of the team and to forget about the 4-S Club for the present time. We were successful in improving the soccer team situation. The team made a *directiva*, agreed on several days for practice, and scheduled several games. Even though I was not successful in organizing the 4-S Club, the soccer team was put in motion. Games were scheduled nearly every week, and the team held raffles to support its endeavors. It was unfortunate that the 4-S Club didn't come to fruition because the youth of Puerto Viejo really needed additional education, as well as the opportunity to learn greater social responsibility.

o   *Caneria* (Potable Water) Project

During my investigation period in Puerto Viejo, it became apparent that the real need of this locale was a *caneria*, a potable water supply. Everyone expressed this as the most urgent concern. After working with Comité Bienstead Comunal, I introduced this idea to the members. They said that it was impractical to begin another project while they were in the process of constructing the community health center. I later tried to interest other members of the community to form a committee pro-caneria.

At the first meeting, only a few people attended; nevertheless, I continually held meetings with five faithful attendees. I later made an appealing invitation, stating that the project was already in focus. One member of the community proposed the idea of making the potable water supply by drilling a well at a nearby spring and buying an automatic pump that would fill the tanks, which would be constructed, twice a day. This proposal seemed feasible and I would present it at the meeting. There was also the idea of making the caneria from a waterfall that was located one and a half kilometers from the center of town. This suggested project also seemed plausible but more expensive.

After having a successful meeting and forming a committee of nine persons, we sent letters to the Municipality of Heredia, requesting an engineer to study the proposals. Shortly afterward, the engineer arrived and investigated the two possible sites. The idea of drilling a well, constructing tanks, and pumping the water was impossible because of insufficient water, and this project would not be prudent from a long-term perspective. The proponent of this method lost enthusiasm in the caneria project, once his idea was rejected. The engineer was impressed with the waterfall scenario and stated that he would send a colleague to perform a topographical study in order to develop an estimated budget. Since the engineer did not come immediately, as was promised, the committee members lost interest and dispersed. Nevertheless, the topographical study was eventually done, and I left the caneria project with the Comité Bienestar Comunal, as I terminated my Peace Corps tour.

This project had some measures of success, yet there were many hindrances. The potable water project was successful from the point of view of community and government relations. The municipality did take an interest in and responded to a project of an isolated community. However, from the perspective of the community, the project was a failure. I realized from the inception that I was doing too much for the project. I had total responsibility. I was cognizant of this when I started organizing the committee. Strategically, I had planned to delegate the responsibility to the committee or one particular member, one I deemed a potential leader. I knew that the committee and the community had the idea that I would get the caneria for them, rather than that they would obtain it for themselves. My only endeavor in this project was to teach the residents that they could and should be instrumental in securing the potable water supply. I knew that I was taking a risk. I rationalized that it was better to attempt in a dismal situation than to resign and say, "It won't work."

Although I was not successful in accomplishing the goal of making the organized committee responsible for the caneria project, I was able to make the community aware that it could be proactive in improving its own destiny. In this project, I realized that Puerto Viejo was extremely limited in its human resources; there were only a few dependable leaders in town. Another factor in the failure of this project was the involvement of the town in the construction of the community health center. During this time the actual work on the center was ongoing. I occupied myself more with the health center because I felt that community development was being accomplished to a greater extent in this project.

During the development of the various projects, I managed to get several community residents to attend seminars organized by the Committee on the Development for Heredia and the National Office of Community Development. These seminars proved to be invaluable educational experiences for these individuals from Puerto Viejo. In the first place, the people of my community had the opportunity to organize and to participate with other communities in this province. It was fascinating to them to learn that other people had similar problems. They had the opportunity to expose the problems of their community to government officials. They felt that an interest had been taken in them. It was quite fortunate that several members of the community attended the seminars because they always returned highly inspired. The seminars were one of the most valuable tools that the Peace Corps and the National Community Development Office had in their long-range policies to improve the lives of individuals in isolated localities.

SITUATION OF COMMUNITY DEVELOPMENT IN PUERTO VIEJO DURING MY TENURE

In existence for about fifteen years, Puerto Viejo, a rural town of approximately eight hundred semi-illiterate individuals, can be reached by highway. Because of the isolation, most people never travel to urban centers, such as Heredia and San Jose. They don't read the newspapers but are informed of the news (*noticias*) by listening to the radio. In order for community development to be more effective, the education level of the people must be increased. Many of the younger population have sixth-grade diplomas, but the older generation, who might have had some schooling earlier, has not continued with habits that would foster the retention of prior studies. In sum, responsiveness to community development requires a certain level of educational awareness. For example, most people refused to work for a common goal because they could not see how they themselves would benefit immediately from the new creation. In Puerto Viejo, specifically, and in the Sarapiqui area, generally, the goals must be mass education. People must be taught to cooperate and to care for each other; in other words, the social and moral standards of the people must be improved in order for community development to be more effective. These factors—lack of preparation, lack of education, and reluctance to cooperate—substantially hindered community development.

There were problems with the leadership in Puerto Viejo. There were few leaders; these leaders of the community were people who had moved into the area within the last few years. In some cases, these "outsiders" were genuinely concerned with the progress of the town, and in other cases, some were only interested in being the bosses. These leaders had dictatorial power and were the most powerful members in the community since there was no governmental control or representation, except the *resguardia* and *policía*. These leaders of the Comité Bienestar Comunal acquired these roles because they were members of the political party that won the last national election. Such individuals refused to do the actual work for a project. Their philosophy was, no matter how small the task might be, a person had to be hired to do the job. In many instances, the committee itself could have performed the task, but these bosses were too haughty to work in this manner.

The committee in general needed more orientation and direction. I realized that was my responsibility, and I attempted to fulfill that role. My endeavors in providing guidance were grossly misinterpreted. My suggesting that there should be periodic financial reports meant that I didn't trust the treasurer. Suggesting that the *junta de educación* (board of education) or the *patronato escolar* (school board) should have meetings meant that I was interfering with the domain of the school director. Suggesting that the *junta edificadora* (the board responsible for construction) should meet and start working to construct the church meant that I was interfering with the plans of the *padre*. In order not to make enemies or create problems, I made suggestions occasionally but would not insist upon pursuing them.

One of the greatest problems that Puerto Viejo had in reference to community development concerned the mission of the Mennonites, who were the first Americans to arrive and live there. They established the initial interactions between Americans and Ticos, which included social, work, and personal relationships. The Mennonites were well accepted and respected, but they never were considered as teachers or leaders; they were cooperators. In other words, they did the work *for* the community rather than *with* the community. Juxtaposed to the Ticos' conception of the Mennonites, a Peace Corps volunteer arrived with a diametrically opposite mission. However, to the local residents, another American had come and, therefore, another Mennonite, whose expected behavior would be consistent with that of the others.

I, however, frequented the salons, intermingled, drank, and danced. "What religion is he? He must be Catholic as we are." These were some of the comments that were made. Nevertheless, after a while, I was able to convince the people that my mission had nothing to do with religion. The relationship the Mennonites established with the Comité Bienestar Comunal made my mission even more challenging. I was thought of as a peon, a laborer, rather than as a coworker. I was to remain quiet during the meetings, just as the Mennonites did. My suggestions were dismissed at the initial phases of my involvement. After a while and after many problems, although there never was any open strife, I gained the confidence of the committee, once my mission was better understood. Originally, I was a threat to their power, but when I realized they had misconstrued my intentions, I immediately let them know that they were the bosses. As a result, in my last few months, my rapport with the committee was superb, and we were able to work together tremendously.

SUMMARY OF PEACE CORPS EXPERIENCE IN COSTA RICA

As a Peace Corps volunteer, I moved from living in the projects in Brooklyn, New York, to working on projects in Puerto Viejo de Sarapiqui, Costa Rica. I also transitioned from living a middle-class lifestyle in San Jose, the capital, to residing in an isolated rural community without many modern amenities, such as running water for bathing and cooking. The Peace Corps enabled me to mature and develop in many ways as I attempted to engage in a humanitarian endeavor. First, I was able to assuage my vehement opposition to the American culture that tolerated racism. Second, I realized, reluctantly, that I am an American because one is a product of his culture and socialization. The Costa Ricans viewed me as an American, just as they viewed Caucasian Americans. I wanted to be considered more African, but that was not in my DNA, from a Tican perspective. Third, I realized my calling as an educator, even though I was trained as a community developer and was participating as such. I always had a disparaging view of teachers. "Those who are not capable of doing anything else became teachers." This was a popular undergraduate philosophy at my institution. Fourth, as I reflect, I realize that I demonstrated leadership capacities not only in my role as a community developer but also as a Peace Corps volunteer in general, as I interacted with other volunteers.

From a humanitarian or Peace Corps perspective, as the first volunteer to Puerto Viejo, I think that I established the relationships with the leading committee and the community, essential for future volunteers. The construction of a local church was a major aspiration. The community would have benefited tremendously from the formation of a 4-S Club. As these concerns have been identified, a future volunteer would have to face the above issues. There were successes in completing the cement bases for the latrines, in initiating the construction of the community-health center, and in getting the local residents to participate in regional and governmental activities that would ultimately benefit their communities. There also were intangible outcomes, such as greater community awareness of the salient problems, more willingness to cooperate on the part of the community in general, and additional leaders eager to assume responsibilities. Even with these limited positive outcomes, I do not regret (and never will regret) my Peace Corps experience and will always cherish it as pivotal in developing the human being I am—someone who is global, cosmopolitan, and eager to learn and explore other cultures without ethnocentrism or xenophobia.

CHAPTER 3

JOURNEY TO THE PROFESSORIATE

After returning from the Peace Corps assignment in Costa Rica in August 1967, I enrolled in the Teachers Corps program at New York University (NYU). NYU was specifically recruiting former Peace Corps volunteers to train to become teachers in the inner-city communities of New York City; the incentive—a tuition-paid master's degree. Even though in my earlier years I never envisioned myself as a teacher, I was attracted to the program because my Peace Corps experience of informally teaching the community English made me realize that I was comfortable imparting knowledge, particularly to children, and that I was well received and appreciated.

I matriculated in the English education program, with a focus in teaching English as a second language. My assignment was in the South Bronx, Alexander Burger Intermediate School, where there was a predominant Spanish-speaking community. My bilingual ability rendered me ideal for this assignment. While I was in this program, Brooklyn College of the City University of New York (CUNY) recruited several of us Teachers Corps interns to teach English skills enrichment to freshman students who would be beginning college in the fall semester. I participated as an instructor in this immersion program during the summers of 1969 and 1970. Based on my performance in teaching these youngsters at Brooklyn College, I was recruited by the program director, Margaret Fulcrum, who was to become the academic development coordinator of the newly founded Medgar Evers College of CUNY, to join her staff.

There were other significant happenings during this time. First was the birth of my son, Kuturi, on December 23, 1970. Second was my job offer to teach in Zambia, Africa. Third was my acceptance to the doctoral program in educational psychology at the Graduate School and University Center of CUNY. After carefully contemplating the above options, I decided to accept the Medgar Evers College (MEC) position, while simultaneously enrolling in the doctor of philosophy (PhD) program.

In the fall of 1971, I became a member of the professoriate, an instructor, and taught reading and writing skills in a collaborative venture with another professor, who taught a content subject. Actually, in the summer of 1971, in a pilot effort, I taught English skills while the content professor taught jazz criticism. We later published a paper, "Jazz Criticism: A Vehicle for Improving Communication Skills," in the *Journal of Jazz Educators*. At the end of my first academic year at MEC (1972), another professor and I accompanied a group of MEC students to Ghana, West Africa. I had always wanted to visit Africa, and I deliberately decided that I would not go as a Peace Corps volunteer because I did not want to go to Africa as a representative of the United States government. At that time, I used to say that I would not rest in peace in my grave if I had not visited Africa, so this opportunity was ideal.

CHAPTER 4

COLLEGE ADVISER TO GHANA

JULY 30, 1972, TO AUGUST 30, 1972

Ghana, which means "black people," is a truly beautiful country. I had been in Ghana for only fifty-eight hours, yet so many wonderful things had happened to me. On the first night, I attended the African Cultural Center, where a show was performed as a welcoming ceremony for Dinizulu and his 250 followers. Dinizulu was an African American who had a dance company and had developed very close ties with Ghanaian cultural groups. What was most intriguing about this event was that black people were talking about oneness, unity, and Pan-Africanism. "Black people throughout the African diaspora" was the theme of conversation. There was very little mention of the differences between African Americans and Africans. The total atmosphere permeated the oneness. Black Americans and African brothers and sisters danced together. Poets mystified the air with their verses. Seeing black people playing drums, dancing rhythmically, and singing harmoniously was indeed an exhilarating experience. I was totally overwhelmed by this welcoming gesture.

Since the students who accompanied the other professor and me were mature men and women, very little supervision was necessary. The students developed their own itineraries and were advised to always travel with at least one companion. One requirement was that they maintain a daily journal, with special emphasis on their reflections of the experiences and interactions in which they engaged. An overwhelming and momentous occasion, such as one's first trip to the homeland, was deliberately structured without major restrictions.

My second day was spent touring Accra and the University of Ghana. I met a young Ghanaian who took me over parts of the vast campus, which consisted of more than one thousand acres. In addition to the numerous departments, there were five different dormitories. There were also a zoo and a botanical garden on this immense campus. Commercially, the university had a bookstore, post office, supermarket, and bank. I was only able to see a relatively small portion of this seemingly limitless campus. To a member of the professoriate from an urban campus, this expansive collegiate environ was phenomenal. Later, my friend and I took the lorry (bus) into Accra.

I had many memorable experiences in Accra during that afternoon, as well as the next few days. I discovered a golf course and was able to practice for a few days. What was most interesting about the golf course was that the putting surface—the green, as we know it—was actually sand. I also visited the national museum and other villages, where I saw fire-eating, skilled drumming, and expert dancing. During these early days in Accra I began to apply for visas to travel to Dahomey, Togo, and Nigeria. One of the major purposes for this additional travel was to visit the slave dungeons, euphemistically called castles, where captured Africans were held until ships arrived to transport them as slaves to the various locales. I was able to secure the visa for Dahomey, but there were delays in obtaining the Togo and Nigeria visas. In the interim, several of the other individuals who had accompanied me on this African trip, having arrived with their visas, made their journeys to those countries I had planned to visit. However, when they returned with such despondent, dejected, and depleted spirits and countenances from visiting the slave dungeons, I concluded that I would not spoil my initial African visit by going to the former slave prison. I would simply spend my total time in Ghana.

After one week in Accra, I took the lorry to Kumasi, the Ashanti region, arriving late in the afternoon. I secured lodging at Hotel de France, a small catering house. Later that evening I went to a local club to socialize. I danced with women and also with men, as that was the custom at the time. There were no homosexual propensities in the Ghanaian men because, culturally, they danced with each other or together. A young man, James Anin, who noticed that I was a stranger, befriended me and invited me to stay at his house. We agreed to make the arrangements the following day. I arrived at his house with my luggage, and what a fabulous house it was. It was a modern two-story brick house with many rooms. He simply wanted to be my host since I was a foreigner in his country. He didn't ask or expect any compensation for his generosity. I met George, Dickerson, and many other of James's brothers; they were all so amicable. Initially, I thought, *How could he have so many brothers?* Then, naively, I deduced that African men could have several wives, and therefore, that explained all those brothers. In reality and from an African perspective, all the brothers were simply his relatives.

Thomas in the background with Ghanain Family

As a host, James wanted to take me to explore many local venues. We toured the market, visited the lake, and went to Kingsway, a neighborhood bar, where I became inebriated from testing the indigenous spirits. In Kumasi, I really became infused within the Ghanaian culture. I was no longer a tourist but one of the members of the local community. I did what the other fellows did, went to places they frequented, and ate the local food, African-style. I had *fufu* for the first time; it consisted of pounded cassava, which looked like kneaded dough, ready for baking, but was served as is. It was eaten by pinching a piece off the lump, dumping it in a stew, and swallowing the fufu with the sauce of the stew. There is no chewing. When I initially had this savory eating experience, I felt full but not satisfied because I didn't masticate. I just had to eat more, so I ate some yams, which required chewing. From this gluttonized venture, I could barely walk and was literally falling asleep on my feet.

Another interesting encounter was the meeting of two African American women at the cultural center. Dorene, a nice-looking, fair-skinned, stoutly built young lady and her companion, also nicely built with wide hips but very dark-skinned, were delighted to meet my friends and me because the local guys could show them the interesting sites in the area; for example, Ashanti New Town, where the girls bought artifacts and other souvenirs. We met the young ladies later in the evening and went dancing at the Star Hotel. I was nonplussed by the attitudes of my friends toward the women. From my cultural orientation, I thought the young men would pursue the nice-looking, fair-skinned one, but no one was interested in her; they all wanted the dark-skinned, voluptuous one. I am certain that these tourists enjoyed their excursion in Kumasi, for the young men treated them royally— teaching them Oware, a Ghanaian board game; taking them to arts-and-crafts shops; and preparing native Ghanaian dishes for them. The above simply exemplifies the positive and beautiful character of the Ghanaians. They were eager to befriend, provide cultural information, and share their resources without expectation of rewards.

Even though I was enjoying Kumasi immensely, I decided that I would travel by lorry to the northern area of the country. On Wednesday, August 9, 1972, I took the bus, filled with friendly, native residents, heading north. In order to reach Tamale, the next major city, one has to cross the Volta River by ferry, but we did not arrive in time to meet the ferry and had to remain on the present side until the following day. I slept in a rest house, accompanied by bats and mice. The next morning, I took the ferry, a comfortable ride, across the Volta, where I saw dead trees in the middle of the river.

Tamale was an interesting town, and I decided to spend a day there while the tour bus continued north. While in Tamale, I met an American couple, Alex and Pat, who were also going to Bolgatanga, the northernmost town, the next day, so I traveled with them. In Bolgatanga, a shopping town, some young boys took us to the market, and I bought, bought, bought, and still was buying when Alex and Pat left me behind. As a result, I had to take the next lorry alone back to Tamale, and I arrived late at night—and had to spend another night at the rest house with my unwelcome nocturnal creatures.

Since I was fascinated with shopping, the next day, while waiting for transport back to Kumasi, I had dashikis made and purchased a large colorful bag. The journey back was a true adventure, as it was a different route by lorry that didn't involve taking the ferry. It was an arduous sixteen-hour ride, with the bus having headlight trouble during the night. Fortunately, we arrived in Kumasi the next morning; I went to James's house, bathed, and had breakfast.

While in Ghana, I had mentioned that I would like to purchase land on the continent; therefore, James decided to take me to a remote village where his brother owned a farm so that I could explore my interest in owning land. James suggested that we purchase some bullets as a gift for his brother. After arriving in Accra, we took a 9:00 p.m. train, a slow but smooth ride, to Tarkwa. Reaching our destination early in the morning, we waited for a bus that would take us to Bolgason, a very small village. From this locale, we had a two-mile walk to James's brother's farm. In that area, land was available for purchase, and I discussed the issues with the elders of the village. We agreed that I would see the land the following day. In the meantime, I met teachers of the village, drank palm wine with them, and discussed relationships between black Americans and Africans. They argued that the white man's attempt was to deceive us both, especially through Christianity. I retired early but had a difficult and restless night on a small bed with a hard mattress and night companions—bed bugs and mosquitoes. Was I glad to get up the next morning!

That morning I was greeted by seeing a small antelope that had been killed by James's brother with the bullets I had brought him. Later, we went to see the land—or forest, as they called it because that was exactly what it was. The land, hilly and soft, was not far from the road; it seemed to have had fertility potential just as other Ghanaian soil. It had a big hole, a well, which supposedly had gold in it. Later in the afternoon, James and I went to Bolgason for a beer after we bathed and swam in the river. Soon afterward we met with the chief and elders to discuss purchasing the land. I was totally impressed with the formality, regality, and sophistication of the meeting. Obviously, I was not able to commit at that time. After the meeting, we returned to Bolgason and then went to Tarkwa. From there, both James and I returned by train; he, to Kumasi and I, to Accra. Incidentally, while in Bolgason, in the middle of nowhere, I could hear music by James Brown blasting loudly from a radio in a domicile.

We had to hire trucks to take us to our respective train stations. I had to wait for hours in the middle of the night for the train. I slept along the wall until the train arrived, but that was better than sleeping on the tiny bed with a hard mattress and suffering incessant mosquito harassment and bites. After traveling third-class, which had the smell of an open market, I arrived at Takoradi and then to Accra.

In Accra, I began to finalize arrangements for shipping the large items I had purchased to New York. I had a large wooden box constructed that would hold two Ashanti stools, two small elephant-shaped night tables, several wooden maps with each African country made of a distinct wood, and other artifacts.

When it was time to depart for home, I was completely overwhelmed from my first African visit. I had seen the beauty of Ghana; I had walked on African soil; I had breathed African air; I had met true African brothers and sisters; and I had interacted with genuine people who expressed solidarity with African Americans. I even learned to have greater love for my own biological family, as well as others, from this African experience. Just as I recommended when I first returned from Ghana that every African American should visit Africa, I still contend the same.

I should also mention that I left my address with my friends in Kumasi, Ghana. Two Ghanaians arrived at different times, and it was my opportunity to reciprocate the hospitality and indulgence that I received from them. Opening my home for them was the least I could do. I returned to Ghana recently, on two different occasions, with one of the individuals I met nearly forty years ago.

CHAPTER 5

PRESENTER AT WORLD CONGRESSES ON COMMUNICATION AND DEVELOPMENT IN AFRICA AND THE AFRICAN DIASPORA, KENYA AND BARBADOS

FIRST CONGRESS—1981

After a red-eye direct flight from John F. Kennedy Airport in New York City to Dakar, Senegal, I placed my feet on African soil once again on July 19, 1981. The flight was not very long, less than seven hours. If one views a world map, one easily can see that Senegal, as it protrudes from northwest Africa, is one of the closest points between the continents of Africa and North America. I was traveling with a group of scholars, primarily college professors, who were also presenting papers at the conference in Nairobi, Kenya. As a complete itinerary, we would spend a few days in each of the following countries: Senegal, Ivory Coast, Nigeria, Kenya, Egypt, and Greece.

On July 20, 1981, I awoke at 8:45 a.m. and jumped out of bed to join the group at 9:00 for a tour of Dakar. My roommate and I took turns using the bathroom for about five minutes each. We didn't take a shower—first, due to the time constraints, and second, because we didn't know we had a shower. We later learned that the faucet from the face basin had an attached cord that interfaced with a clamp above the bathtub to provide water for the shower. However, we did just make the bus for the tour. We had a guide, Segnha, who spoke English relatively well and was able to tell us some of the historical features of the country, as well as cultural aspects. We saw the University of Senegal, the fabulous houses of the ambassadors, and several local markets, including the artisan market, where there were many types of handicrafts, solid gold, and a lot of ivory. I didn't buy anything because I felt that I had overdone it the day before. At the silversmith market, operated primarily by Mauritanians, I almost purchased some silver but reneged at the final moment.

After the tour, my roommate and I had lunch on the sixth floor at the Independence Hotel in downtown Dakar. There was a lovely view of the city from the restaurant. I ate salad, rice, and fish and drank some wine. Later that afternoon we went by ferry to the island of Goree, which was a place that maintained a former slave dungeon—holding cells for captured Africans until the next ship arrived to transport them to a life of misery and degradation. It is mystifying how a prison for slaves could be called a slave "castle." It is incredulous that people could treat other people in such an inhumane manner. The cells had very small windows, through which many people tried to obtain air. The windows were tiny so the captured people could not crawl through them and escape. The spaces were grossly inadequate for the large number of people who were literally packed into them. Hooks still remained that were used to turn people upside down if they had diarrhea. I had an eerie sensation that I still could feel the pain and agony of my ancestors who had endured this horrific treatment. As I was leaving the island I gave my Toronto Blue Jays cap to a little boy who had become fascinated with it. We left the island, sad and dejected, and returned to the hotel. Later that evening, I ate Chinese food, drank a couple of beers, and went to bed.

On July 21, 1981, I had the continental breakfast at the hotel, exchanged money, and left for a trip by taxi with other travelers. We visited Rufisque en route to Thies. In Thies, we visited the market, and it was an exciting experience. Later, we went to the National Manufactory of Tapestry. The museum was fantastic, with beautiful, exotic prints and tapestries. I bought a print of a Senegalese woman, which I would later frame and place in my living room back home. On the journey back to Dakar, we stopped for mangoes and to photograph the baobab tree. These trees have their own unique shapes and individual personalities. Upon arriving back at the hotel and resolving the fare for the trip, my roommate and I relaxed by having a couple of beers. Later that evening we all went to Amadu's house for dinner, which was a huge basin of a national dish made with rice, fish, yams, yucca, hot peppers, and other seasonings. Such food was delicious, especially when eaten African-style; that is, with the hands from a communal bowl. After dinner, we danced until about eleven thirty. Then it was back to the hotel to retire after an adventurous day.

On the following morning, we departed at eight thirty for the airport. After waiting for three hours and arranging our travel affairs, we left on a flight to Abidjan, Ivory Coast, and arrived there at 2:15 p.m. As we left the airport, we took a tour of the sites of this beautiful, exquisite city, including the market; the museum, where the pieces were extraordinary; and the crafts area, where I wished we could have spent more time. I did purchase an ivory bracelet for fourteen dollars. Then we checked in at a very nice hotel. For dinner, I went with several members of the group to seek a place where local native food was served. Initially, we stopped at an open corner where fish was being cooked in front of our very eyes. There were benches and small tables for us to use; of course, there were no eating utensils, napkins, or plates. We had the choice of eating inside the cook's house or, if we wanted to take the food out, eating it wrapped in banana leaves. These arrangements were much too ethnic for most of the group, so we decided to go to another restaurant that had an African ambience but European overtones.

After dinner, we visited the Hotel Ivoire, which was an exclusive complex within itself. It must have been designed for millionaires. There were many shops and boutiques that had the finest of African wares, as well as exquisite items from all parts of the world. We simply had a tour of this pricey establishment and departed, worrying about how we were going to pay the taxi fare.

After just one day, we had to leave the beautiful Abidjan so hurriedly. Our flight to Lagos, Nigeria, was scheduled for 8:30 a.m. I almost forgot my attaché case, which contained my paper that I was to present at the conference and other related materials. We had no problems at the airport, as prearrangements had been made. At ten o'clock we departed for Lagos.

NIGERIA

In Nigeria, I recall two major events. One was a trip by bus from Lagos to the University of Nigeria in Ibadan. As we traveled on the highway I noticed Nigerian soldiers with assault rifles standing at various stations. Then, to my surprise, the bus stopped, and soldiers entered the bus, brandishing their weapons. It was considered a routine security check, but I was scared to death. No one was harmed, and we were allowed to proceed, but the shock remained with me as we entered and toured the university. The other event etched in my memory was an invitation for dinner at the home of a Nigerian dignitary (a politician). He lived in a very affluent neighborhood; all the houses appeared to be mansions. We had drinks and hors d'oeuvres before dinner, and, for the first time, I had escargot, which was considered a delicacy comparable to caviar. The dinner was excellent and the conversation intriguing, but all I could remember was tasting a gritty snail.

KENYA

I was excited to arrive in Nairobi, Kenya, where the conference would be held. The First World Congress on Communication and

Development in Africa and the African Diaspora was an international showcase of Pan-African scholars who were eager to present their ideas and solutions to myriad problems that existed among the peoples of African descent. It was intellectually stimulating to be in the midst of such intelligentsia. I presented my research paper, derived from my dissertation, "Communication Skills in the Inner City: Effects of Race and Dialect on Decoding," and it was well received. Yet it didn't compare with the visionaries who proposed solutions to economic, social, and political issues that permeated the African third-world countries.

While in Nairobi I observed a rather intriguing phenomenon. During the day, the streets were filled with varied commercial activities. There was a lot of traffic: trucks delivering merchandise, cars and bicycles going in all directions, and people on the streets, shopping. This seemed like certain areas in midtown Manhattan, New York. At night, however, Nairobi was the diametric opposite of the activities in New York City. Early in the evening all the shops closed. There was practically no traffic on the streets, and there were no people in sight. What had been a thriving, bustling city hours earlier now appeared to be a deserted town. The Europeans and Asians went to their residential areas, while the native Kenyans went to their suburban townships, thereby explaining the empty metropolis. The few local Kenyans who remained to socialize in the bars and taverns later would have to take taxis to their homes on the outskirts of Nairobi.

One evening, several of the other male travelers and I met some ladies at a bar. Obviously, we were out to enjoy the evening with female companionship. We secured a table, ordered beer for everyone—liter-size and at room temperature was preferred—and engaged in conversation. These young ladies, who were not educated and had jobs as domestics, were well informed on international affairs and rather inquisitive about American lifestyles and politics. The social intercourse was engaging and enlightening. For example, I wanted to know the young ladies' tribal affiliation, whether Kikuyu or some other tribes, but they simply stated that they were Kenyans, thereby reinforcing the national resolve of not allowing tribal identification to separate them. They wanted to understand more precisely from us the dynamics between black and white Americans. At the end of the evening, instead of viewing the women as romantic experiences, we men considered them more as sisters.

EGYPT AND GREECE

Before returning to the States, we made stops in Cairo, Egypt, and Athens, Greece. It was marvelous to see the Valley of the Kings, the Sphinx, and the pyramids. I examined closely the massive stones that comprised the pyramids and could see how each stone was strategically placed on the other without mortar or cement to form these amazing structures. When I entered a pyramid, stepping out of the scorching heat outdoors, I found it incredible that the temperature inside was cool, as if there were air conditioning. Also, while in Cairo, I had to see the Nile. So I went to the mouth of the Nile, took my shoes off, and dipped my feet into this iconic river.

Dr. Edwards posing in front of the Sphinx

When we arrived in Athens and went sightseeing, the first things I saw—and couldn't believe they actually were there—were watermelons. Then we saw the Hellenic ruins—history coming alive before my very eyes. From the top of some structures, we could see below where the arenas probably were. It was astonishing to carefully examine the ruins and imagine how such magnificence was constructed so many years earlier. Since Athens is on the Mediterranean, of course I had to dip my feet in that sea. I may not have left footprints in the sand or crossed the Jordan, but my feet were baptized in the Nile River and the Mediterranean Sea.

Thomas cooling his feet in the Mediterranean Sea.

SECOND CONGRESS

BARBADOS, 1983

Another scholarly presentation that involved travel was the Second World Congress on Communication and Development in Africa and the African Diaspora, which was held in Barbados, West Indies. My topic was "Different States of Consciousness in Speaking Standard English versus Dialect." In this linguistic discourse, I posited that standard English has evolved from a Eurocentric worldview, whereas black English, a dialect, has its roots in an African view of the world. Social philosopher Frantz Fanon (1957) stated, "Every dialect is a way of thinking ..." When people of African ancestry speak a dialect, the Afrocentric worldview or African philosophy is as much a part of the utterances as the words; hence, the oral tradition and call-and-response behavior. For example, a preacher would expect an "Amen" from his audience. Furthermore, the concern of the community, which remains in most people of African ancestry, is an important aspect of Afrocentric philosophical orientation. On the other hand, standard English, emanating from a Eurocentric worldview, positions the individual as the center of attention; therefore, the terms survival of the fittest, rugged individualism, and capitalism. The Eurocentric perspective, stemming from the Greco-Roman tradition, which separates mind from body, is the diametric opposite of the Afrocentric philosophical notion that the mind and body are one. In sum, there are different mental processes utilized in speaking standard English and black English, thereby the existence of two different states of consciousness that have their origins in Eurocentric and Afrocentric worldviews, respectively. It also should be noted that whereas my presentation at the First World Congress in Kenya involved research and actual data, the presentation at the Second World Congress was a conceptual and theoretical exposé.

When my colleagues and I were returning to the United States from Barbados, we had a fortuitous experience. The flight was overbooked, and some passengers from the coach section were upgraded to first class; several of us were the lucky ones. I had never flown first class before that time, so I just sat back, relaxed, and enjoyed all the accoutrements. I ordered drinks continually, ate choice delicious food, and relished my pampered status, all for free. The travel and scholarly presentation in Barbados, a serene and peaceful island, was successful in more ways than one.

CHAPTER 6

ORGANIZER AND PRESENTER AT INTERNATIONAL AFRICAN AMERICAN CULTURAL AND RESEARCH ASSOCIATION CONFERENCES IN BRAZIL,1988

I n the early months of 1987, a group of individuals—including Professor Matthew Meade, several Brazilians, and I—began meeting at Medgar Evers College after work hours to plan a trip to Brazil for the following year to commemorate the centennial of Brazil's "Emancipation Proclamation." It should be noted that this freedom from slavery occurred twenty-five years after the so-called liberation in the United States. Underlying the impetus of this travel project was the desire to develop close relationships between African Americans and African Brazilians. We met regularly and tirelessly in this endeavor. After a great deal of brainstorming, we decided to name our group the "International African American Cultural and Research Association" (IAACRA) The term *international African American* encompasses all persons of African ancestry who reside in the Western Hemisphere. The mission of IAACRA is to improve and foster intergroup relations and cultural exchanges among all people, especially those of African origin. We finalized our plans for the 1988 travel and agreed that we would have an itinerary that would include touring Rio de Janeiro and Salvador, in the state of Bahia, where the scholarly conference would be held. More specifically, we solicited papers centered around the theme, Commemorating the One Hundredth Anniversary of the Abolition of Slavery in Brazil: the Media and the African American/African Brazilian. The conference included speakers from both the United States and Brazil and was held at the Federal University of Bahia, August 16–20, 1988. The late Dr. Betty Shabazz, widow of Malcolm X, was the keynote speaker for this momentous occasion. Some of the titles of the papers presented were "A Historical Analysis of Racism in Brazil"; "A Estetica da Cidadania: Discriminação no Surgimento do Estado Moderno no Brasil, 1881/1889" (The Aesthestics of Citizenship: Racial Discrimination in the Resurgence of the Modern State in Brazil, 1881/1889); and "Trade Deficits in Brazil and the United States." Bahia was selected as the venue for the conference because this Brazilian state has the largest concentration of Brazilians of African descent. Actually, a world map shows that Bahia is one of the closest distances between South America and Africa.

The conference was the highlight of this travel, but we also spent time visiting the tourist sites and participated in major cultural events that occurred during our stay. We saw Sugar Loaf Mountain and Cristo Redentor (the gigantic statue of Jesus Christ) on Corcovado Mountain in Rio. We experienced the parade, *Boa Morte*, where elderly African Brazilian women, dressed in traditional regalia (supposedly a secret society), carry a statue of the Virgin Mary through the streets from a particular locale to a designated church. This event seems to represent a synchronism between Candomblé, a traditional African religion, and Catholicism. We also met with local Brazilian groups, some Afrocentric; others militant and progressive. At that time, however, there was very little identity with Africa among Brazilians of African ancestry.

As a founder of IAACRA, I was extremely content with the success of our first venture. We increased our knowledge of our Brazilian brothers and sisters, and they, likewise, gained greater understanding, firsthand, of African Americans. For example, as we explained the scope and mission of our association, several Brazilians asked, "If you are focused on African (black) Americans, then why do you have a white woman in your group?" The white woman was a very fair-skinned "sister." We had to explain that, ethnically and culturally, she too was African American. Similarly, we had to comprehend that Brazilians didn't categorize themselves as blacks and whites, but there were numerous designations based on skin color and hair texture. Two persons with similar skin color but different hair texture would be placed in different categories. The complexity of identity among African Brazilians intrigued me, and I subsequently did research on the issue, as you will see below in the discussion of my Fulbright scholars project.

We returned to Brazil from August 14 to August 31, 1989, for part two of "IAACRA Presents": "The Media and the African American and the African Brazilian." The conference and tour of Rio de Janeiro, as well as tours of the federal and Catholic universities of Bahia in Salvador, were an extension of the first trip. Dr. Betty Shabazz was gracious enough to accompany us again and serve as keynote speaker. We visited historic sites, festivals, arts-and-crafts fairs, and religious communities. We had meetings with Brazilian scholars and artists, utilizing bilingual assistance as needed. We even began discussion of faculty and student exchanges, which did come to fruition several years later.

Dr. Edwards participating in Boa Morte Festival in Bahia, Brazil.

CHAPTER 7

FULBRIGHT-HAYS GROUP STUDY ABROAD PROGRAM IN BRAZIL, JUNE 24–JULY 31, 1994

I was a participant in the Morehouse College/Georgia International Education Consortium Project, which was one of the most gratifying and professionally rejuvenating experiences of my career. I will present the results of my project here. It begins with a narrative of my activities in Brazil from June 24 to July 31, 1994, followed by a summary of the results of my individual project, "Self-Identity among African Brazilians." Finally, I will highlight the implementation of my experience and research in Brazil into a cross-cultural psychology course that I teach. As stated above, there are personal, professional, and educational components in the summary of this report.

NARRATIVE

After four days of orientation in Atlanta, Georgia, from June 20 through June 23, 1994, I was eagerly anticipating the journey to Brazil.

The Atlanta orientation was quite informative, particularly in delineating what our responsibilities were and what our expectations should be as we interacted in the study-abroad seminar. The presentation in curriculum development was outstanding, and the language instruction served as a foundation for those who were adventuresome and unafraid to attempt to communicate in the host language. Therefore, on Thursday evening, June 23, 1994, I enthusiastically boarded the plane for the long flight to Brazil.

SAO PAULO

We arrived in Sao Paulo on Friday, June 24, at approximately 6:00 a.m., local time. Since we were Fulbright scholars and previous arrangements had been made in expectation of our arrival, there were no hassles whatsoever at customs. As we left the airport, our tour guide, Walter, a mature gentleman, told us about Sao Paulo and its inhabitants, industries, and pollution. What was disgustingly revolting was the sight of the Tietê River, which ran parallel to the highway from the airport to the center of town. Walter talked about the polluted river nonchalantly as he lectured us on how the rich in Brazil were getting richer, while the poor were getting poorer. According to Walter, the poor were unable to get into the university because they attended inferior schools and couldn't pass the entrance examination.

The smog from the factories hovered over the city, and all the buildings in sight looked dingy. Walter stated that the Brazilian government had requested funds from the World Bank, and, in fact, the World Bank was planning to lend the money so that the waste and smog would be cleaned up before the twenty-first century. To me, this was a graphic illustration of how multinational corporations and the wealthy of Brazil destroy the environment by making it unhealthy for all, especially the poor, and, in the process, the rich get richer. Of course, this is done with government sanctioning. Perhaps this helps to understand the corruption that is pervasive in the Brazilian government. The bottom line is that the rest of the world has to pay to clean up the environment that the rich have polluted and destroyed, thereby causing health problems for the citizens of Sao Paulo. Walter also discussed the politics of Brazil, particularly, the upcoming elections.

Shortly after ten o'clock, after checking in the hotel and having the buffet breakfast, I witnessed all sorts of Paulista (of Sao Paulo) activities, such as a man entertaining a small crowd by walking a tightrope, performing karate, and juggling (You name it; he was doing it.) What I observed was the audience—men primarily but some women—of all colors, who were watching the tricks and listening to the jokes of this character. Farther along the walk were two young men who were engaged in other stunts; for example, jumping through a mounted circle that had long nails protruding from the circumference toward the center. Then I listened to a woman who was demonstrating how human reproduction occurred while simultaneously selling an aphrodisiac. (Incidentally, at the end of the other two demonstrations mentioned above, the performers also sold products.) This was my first opportunity to interact with the people of Sao Paulo. They were not very attractive people, aesthetically speaking, and many seemed to be marginalized.

In the afternoon, after the orientation meeting and a short rest, I went to see the *futbol* (soccer) game between Brazil and Cameroon. This was during the World Cup tournament, and the competition was shown on a very large screen in the midst of a plaza. A vast crowd of people were there. When Brazil scored the first goal, the crowd yelled, waved Brazilian flags, and set off fireworks. There is nothing like the frenzy Brazilians display when their team plays and scores. After the first score, I left with my colleagues, and we had dinner. Later, we walked around, crossing a nearby bridge, and saw many homeless persons. This sparked a discussion about our project, and we stood outside the hotel for a couple of hours, expressing our views of African Americans, African Brazilians, and environmental and health issues.

SATURDAY, JUNE 25, 1994

I awoke around seven o'clock to prepare for a trip to Holambra. This day was rainy and cold. After having breakfast, we boarded the bus for the trip, along with the Tougaloo College group, another Fulbright-Hays study-abroad group that was examining cultural issues in Brazil. As we rode, we saw the countryside, and tour guide, Walter, gave us some information about the sites and the country in general. The word *Holambra* was derived from the first few letters of Holland, America, and Brazil; it denotes that this community, developed by immigrants from Holland, received the assistance of both the American and Brazilian governments. At the particular locale that we visited, there was a photographic museum that preserved the history of the Dutch people in Brazil. One shocking photograph was of several Dutch Brazilians masquerading as blacks. Most of the African Americans found this depiction offensive. The curator of the museum attempted to explain that the scene in the photograph was part of an annual celebration to show the children that Pedro Negro, the disguised black person, would "get" them if they misbehaved. Otherwise, there was no malicious intent involved.

Later, we had lunch at the Holambra Restaurant. When we left, we drove near coffee plantations that were operated by the Japanese, who had migrated to Brazil after World War II. When we returned to the hotel, we had a short briefing before dinner. In the evening, several of us participants went to Lumbar, a nightclub. The crowd was very young and vibrant, and the dance was the lambada, lambada, and lambada. However, even though most of us did not dance the lambada, the evening was enjoyable. Incidentally, the young clientele consisted of individuals of all races and colors, and they intermingled completely.

The early part of the following week consisted of visits to the open markets in Sao Paulo where we shopped for curios and souvenirs. The activity of haggling over the price of items afforded me the opportunity to practice using the little Portuguese I was learning. Since we, Fulbright scholars, were now interacting with the people of Brazil and learning more about their culture, we began to discuss our individual projects from a more pragmatic perspective. During this time, we visited the Biological Institute (operated by the Federal University of Sao Paulo). There we saw and examined specimens of various animals and their diseased appearances. What was noticeable was that the equipment used in this lab seemed antiquated. After we viewed the items in the museum, there was a video presentation and discussion. The general focus of the exchanges was how diseased plants and animals affect the environment. We also examined some of the coffee that was grown there. I was truly surprised to see coffee plants as high as twelve and thirteen feet. This contrasts with coffee plants I had seen previously in Costa Rica, which were only about five feet in height. After leaving the Biological Institute, we visited a coffee-processing plant, Café Do Ponto Industry. There, we saw a video of how coffee is grown and processed. Later, we toured the processing plant to see how coffee was prepared for the market and for consumption. We were all given a generous gift—many samples of coffee, including gourmet varieties.

TUESDAY, JUNE 28, 1994

The activities of the day were exciting indeed. We departed early in the morning to visit an open school operated by an African Brazilian couple, Zulma and Jose Luis. The purpose of this school was to provide education for homeless children. Two groups of children were serviced by this school, as there was a morning and an afternoon session. It was fantastic to see children—clean, well mannered, and courteous. They enjoyed our presence as well. We discussed with our host the philosophy of the school and its goals and objectives. Issues related to African Brazilians and African Americans consistently entered our dialogue. We had a scrumptious lunch there. As the school was sponsored by the Ba'hai religion, we were invited to a reception later in the week at the Ba'hai Institute. As we left the school it was heartwarming to say good-bye to the children, who tried to utilize their English knowledge.

Before returning to Sao Paulo, we stopped at a historic town, Itui, where we strolled around, shopped, and had refreshments. The trip back to the hotel was uneventful, but I was glad to return after a full day of activities.

WEDNESDAY, JUNE 29, 1994

Today was a day in which there were optional activities. Some of the group rented a car to travel to Santos, a town in the south of Sao Paulo close to an area called Cuperton, where there was a great amount of pollution. Others decided to take the subway to the mall. After returning from the mall, we met several professional African Brazilians who were friends of a friend of one of the Fulbright scholars. These persons were Dr. Silvo Luis de Oliveria, director of international affairs for the Universidade Alberto Do Brasil; Ana Maria Do Nascimento de Oliveria, consultant for special affairs at the same university; Pedro Paulo Ananias Pio, manager of the division, Department of Investment of the Bank of the State of Sao Paulo; and Umberto Elias Agiar Sertorio, a dental surgeon. These individuals invited us to participate in a cultural exchange dialogue at the Open University of Brazil.

THURSDAY, JUNE 30, 1994

Today, Willie, another scholar, and I decided to go to Cuperton ourselves to see the pollution. The program planned for the day was canceled, although there was a group meeting scheduled for five o'clock that evening. We initially considered taking the subway to the southernmost point; then we inquired about the bus schedule to Santos. After several miscues, we finally embarked on our journey. The ride was approximately ninety minutes. Once we arrived, we discovered that we had to take another bus to Cuperton. The time prohibited us from going directly to Cuperton, as we were concerned about the return bus schedule and arriving back to Sao Paulo in order to be punctual for the group meeting. However, the trip was not in vain, as we saw instances of pollution and hazardous waste along the roadside as we traveled to Santos.

Santos is a coastal town with lovely beaches and beautiful luxury condominiums. Even though we did not get a close-up view of the environmental waste and pollution caused by the oil industry in this area, the journey was worthwhile and rewarding. After the group meeting, in which we discussed our progress and future plans, we met three young men who had come to the hotel as guests of one of our scholars. These individuals represented the Unified Black Movement (Movimento Unificado Negro). We were able to get insightful information about the perspectives of African Brazilians who recognized the racism and discrimination against them. They labeled the phrase, "Brazil is a racial democracy," as a myth. Participation in this discussion was an excellent way to end the day.

FRIDAY, JULY 1, 1994

We had our tour of Sao Paulo. It was ironic that we had the city tour at the end of our stay in Sao Paulo. Nevertheless, we did see several interesting sites during this early morning venture. In the afternoon, it was rest time and preparation for an invited dinner for the entire group at the Ba'hai Institute. This was organized by Zulma and Jose Luis. The food was exotic but excellent. Before dinner, we spent time introducing ourselves and discussing our professions and specific projects. I was bold enough to attempt my introduction in Portuguese. The host gathering applauded enthusiastically after my hesitant, inarticulate Portuguese, but I was ecstatic about the response. The Ba'hai members also introduced themselves, and many of them spoke English fluently. They were of all races and colors but primarily Caucasian and East Indian. We learned about the philosophy of the Ba'hai: true brotherhood among all peoples of the world and the expansiveness of the religion, which I was hearing about for the first time.

After dinner, we intermingled and discussed cultural exchanges. I also presented Zulma and Jose Luis with a two- hundred dollars donation, which was collected from the Fulbright scholars to be used for the homeless children at the school. It was my idea to make such a gesture, as I was truly moved by the interaction with the children and the noble work of Zulma and Jose Luis. I also met an African Brazilian, Francisco Marcos Dias, an engineer at the Department of Infrastructure and Support in the transportation system. We discussed many items, cultural and racial in particular. He also agreed to attend the program the next day at the Universidade Alberta do Brasil. Indeed, the evening was an enriching and stimulating one.

SATURDAY, JULY 2, 1994

Saturday was a quiet day in its entirety. We left the hotel at approximately 9:45 a.m. to go to the Universidade Alberta do Brasil at MacKenzie. Several of the hosts met us at the hotel, and we traveled by both bus and car. At the school, we had an introductory session and were welcomed by school officials and the persons who organized the meeting. This school's nontraditional approach offered many Brazilians an opportunity for higher education. I was delighted to see what appeared to be a greater concentration of African Brazilians at this university.

We later separated into smaller groups with Paulistas (Brazilians) and Fulbright scholars convening according to similar professions, in order to discuss issues related to our concept papers. For example, some information presented included the fact that there are sixty million African Brazilians, 40 percent of the population; the lowest index of poverty is within this group; and Brazil is the ninth greatest industrial country in the world. The desire to develop a continuous exchange between the United States professionals and the Brazilians was also expressed. In my particular group, we discussed mental health issues, especially as they related to the African Brazilian population. There is a need for therapy for many African Brazilians, yet they have a negative attitude toward psychotherapy. African Brazilians deny their history, have low self-esteem, and don't take pride in themselves. Finally, there is the fact that Brazilian black professionals do not assume any major responsibility in assisting other blacks.

During this time, I was able to complete the writing of the questions for my survey that I wanted to ask professionals and laity alike. Several of the individuals translated the questions into Portuguese for me. When the questions were completed, I was able to administer the survey to four individuals. Consequently, I made fantastic strides toward completing the project in my concept paper. Without doubt, this event was the highlight of my experience in Sao Paulo.

We later decided to continue the dialogue by having lunch together. We went to a barbeque restaurant where customers could eat all the meat they wanted—beef, pork, chicken, and so on. I was noncarnivorous at the time, so can you imagine me at such a place? There was no fish or other seafood. We grouped ourselves with other Brazilians, those who were not in our group at the university, and continued our discussion. Again, these activities, which ended around 4:30 p.m., were most productive. We returned to the hotel and prepared for an evening out at a reggae nightclub. The music was reggae and more reggae; it was great fun. Then, it was to bed at approximately 2:30 a.m. The bus departure for Rio de Janeiro was scheduled for 7:00 a.m.

RIO DE JANEIRO

SUNDAY, JULY 3, 1994

We were en route to Rio de Janeiro at the scheduled time. The bus was comfortable, and we took the scenic roads, passing through a mountainous area from Sao Paulo, then through the interior to Caraguatatuba, and onward to Ubatuba, which led us down the mountains to the coastal region. This journey was extremely picturesque, as we could see the Atlantic Ocean. Most interesting was that as we passed the rural areas, we could see tiny houses that in some cases were dilapidated, yet there were the satellite dishes on many of them. We stopped for lunch at Parity, a small seaport town that catered to tourists. First, we walked around and saw some of the articles on sale in shops and on the streets. Afterward, we had lunch at a very nice restaurant while sitting outside beside the river that flowed through the town. The food was excellent, seafood primarily.

We continued the journey, which was uneventful, with the exception of a few jolting bumps on the road. In some areas, the roads were in need of repair. We arrived in Rio at approximately 6:45 p.m. and checked into a small hotel on the Copacabana Beach. Several of us were so excited, rather than being exhausted from the long ride—the excitement attributed to experiencing an atmosphere different from drab Sao Paulo—that we went out to dinner at a Chinese restaurant and then walked along the beach. The most shocking sights during this time of night, besides several homeless persons, were the transvestites and prostitutes. (Prostitution is legal in Rio.) I retired at around eleven thirty, alone, of course.

MONDAY, JULY 4, 1994

At nine o'clock in the morning we had a group meeting to discuss the itinerary and other plans for Rio. Later, we accepted an invitation to tour Sterns, a gemstone industry. We were picked up by cars and taken to Sterns, where we saw how gemstones are developed and refined. After the tour, we were asked to visit the showroom and, of course, to purchase exclusive Brazilian gemstones and gold. Then we were free for the remainder of the day.

I had lunch, buffet-style, at the Meredian Hotel and later returned to see the soccer game—Brazil versus the United States on the Fourth of July. In Brazil, the game itself was tantamount to our celebration of Independence Day; firecrackers went off whenever Brazil scored.

The entire country shut down during the match. All the shops closed, and there practically were no cars on the roads. When Brazil emerged victorious, there was a parade down the main streets and partying at the plazas. The television channels discussed nothing but the victory. All the Brazilians were wildly excited about the game, but we Americans could not have cared less. Once the game was over, normal activities resumed, but the conversation was only about the triumph.

TUESDAY, JULY 5, 1994

As I entered the dining room for breakfast, I met Dr. Lun Chin Chow, an evaluator of the Fulbright program from the United States Department of Education. We had a brief conversation related to the Morehouse College Fulbright project.

Since this was a free day, I accepted an invitation to visit another jewelry dealer, Moreno's. I was interested in visiting this area because it was near the hotel, Rio Orthon Palace, where I had stayed when I visited Rio in 1988 and 1989. The nostalgia was overwhelming because my now-estranged wife had accompanied me on the prior trips. This was the only time that I really seemed to miss her in the almost three years of separation. Later in the afternoon, I had dinner alone at a local restaurant. I enjoyed eating at places where the ordinary people dined. I thought I was ordering fish fillet, but I was given beef, which I had to return. Of course, my initial order was in Portuguese, as well as my reorder for fish, which I did receive.

WEDNESDAY, JULY 6, 1994

Our first appointment was with Secretary of Health (*Secretario Municipal de Salud*) Ronaldo Luiz Galla. At his office, he provided information about the Brazilians' health status, especially contrasting health care in the United States to that in Brazil. For example, he stated that 80 percent of the United States population had health insurance, while 80 percent of the Brazilian population had no health coverage. In Brazil, seventy dollars per capita was spent for health care, whereas in the United States, $2,400 per capita was spent. Some of the major problems faced by Brazilians were infant mortality, hypertension, traffic accidents, urban violence, AIDS, and tuberculosis. Of the 150 million people in Brazil, 30 million suffered from malnutrition and 2.5 million were starving. It seemed to me that more could have been done to improve the general population if the desire were there. Since the majority of the poor and forgotten were people of color, particularly descendants of former slaves, there was no major interest in investing resources into these marginalized human beings.

The next appointment in the same building was with Secretaria Municipal de Educacao, Regina de Assis. However, we first spoke to her staff member Iza Locatelli, director of teaching. She informed us about the educational structure in the city of Rio de Janeiro, the number of students (700,000), and the number of teachers (35,000). We had a general discussion about how education affects politics by teaching environmental awareness and cultural diversity.

"We want black students to be proud of being black and not have self-hatred or value white standards," stated the speaker. School clubs were formed also to keep children around the school and not in the streets. Other issues such as environmental education—namely, recovering and recycling, use of museums in instruction, and institutes for the physically disabled—also were discussed.

Later, we did meet with Dr. Assis, the municipal secretary of education. She was well informed about education in the United States and agreed to write and jointly publish with one of the Fulbright scholars. As we left the building we were swamped by demonstrators—teachers who were on strike for better wages and working conditions. Several of them cornered us near our van and began a barrage of questions and comments. They informed us that their average salary was $125 per month and that the educational officials with whom we had just spoken might say how grand and noble the curriculum was, yet there were no resources, such as books and material, to implement it. This visit resulted in a plethora of information regarding health care, education concerns, and disenchanted teachers.

Later in the afternoon, after our return to the hotel, I went for a walk in the neighborhood and to find a restaurant. I enjoyed being by myself at times, to reflect and to develop greater solidarity with the Brazilian populace. In the evening, starting at eight thirty, we had a meeting with Dr. Chow to discuss her observations of the Morehouse College Fulbright scholars.

THURSDAY, JULY 7, 1994

A visit to the Secretaria Extraordinaria de Defensa e Promocao das Populacoes Afro-Brasilerias (SEAFRO) was the first activity of the day. There, we conversed with Carlos Alberto Mediros, one of the directors at SEAFRO. He explained the objectives of this agency—to promote laws that fight racial discrimination, to change the roles played by blacks in society, and to change the curriculum in public schools; that is, to Africanize it. We also discussed the psychological conflict that many African Brazilians experienced; most of them identified themselves as being mixed, an attempt to deny their African heritage. Later, Mr. Mediros introduced us to his supervisor, who had just arrived, Abdias Do Nascimento, the noted Brazilian author and scholar.

No one in the group seemed to have recognized him, so I mentioned that I was familiar with some of his writings. At that point he pulled from under his table a number of his books, including *Africans in Brazil, Sortilege Crosswinds: An Anthology of Black Dramatists in the Diaspora*, and *O Quilombismo*. Mr. Do Nascimento spoke about his struggle to bring greater African consciousness within the Brazilian population, while simultaneously advocating projects of affirmative action in the armed forces, police department, and the work force. There was also the fight to maintain an ecological museum related to the African Brazilian experience, a specific area of turf reserved for rituals in the Tijuca Forest in Rio de Janeiro. Other aspects of the conversation centered around the themes of several of his books. This was a very enlightening morning. I even realized that I could understand a considerable amount of the discussion in Portuguese.

After having lunch in the vicinity, we boarded the van, driven by Claudia, a young woman who could really handle that vehicle. Off we went to Programa Negritude Brasilera (PNB), an organization involved with social interventions from an anthropological perspective. Furthermore, it conducts research on religion and religiosity, provides technical assistance to other organizations, and is intricately involved with Candomblé, the African (Yoruba) religion that is still practiced throughout Brazil. We saw a video focusing on how health problems, such as AIDS, are dealt with using Candomblé. The speaker mentioned the different African languages that are used in Candomblé, and I inquired if these languages were spoken by the participants on occasions other than the religious ceremonies. As I have always had a psycholinguistic interest in Brazil, I was chagrined to hear the response was negative. We even talked about the various *orishas* or gods (spirits) that people worshipped in Candomblé. I found it intriguing that a Brazilian could practice Candomblé and at the same time be a devoted Catholic. There are no inconsistencies in this religious duality. In sum, this organization used religion to promote health and the general welfare of Brazilians. I was truly fascinated with the total exposures of the day.

FRIDAY, JULY 8, 1994

Our initial appointment was with the *Secretaria De Meio Ambiente* (Secretary of Environment) Alfredo Sirkis of the municipal government of the city of Rio de Janeiro. Mr. Sirkis spoke fluent English and explained to us the function of his office. The new constitution of 1988 created the environmental agency, and what previously was a federal government responsibility became under the aegis of the city.

Maintaining a viable urban ecology was the most important task, and there were three coordinated departments: (1) environmental control, which was responsible for inspecting the environment, forestation, both water and air pollution, and illegal construction in protected areas; (2) environmental recovery, which attempted to refurbish through reforestation and improve the water, air, and soil; and (3) planning, which monitored the city by environmental education. There also were regional offices to address environmental issues. Two foundations maintained the parks, gardens, urban trees, and the zoo. The basic concept of these foundations was that protecting the environment was a task of the public, and their efforts were integrated with other entities, such as the federal, state, and local governments. This municipal environmental office also had several involvements with the business sector. However, there were clashes with bus companies because they did not adhere to the environmental standards to control air pollution. Many developers who were not environmentally concerned also posed many problems. Since a major conference in 1992, the business sectors changed somewhat—the environment was important to them as citizens and as business people.

Several of the major problems of the environment were identified. Water was the main problem. There were many areas of Rio de Janeiro without running water, and as a result of not having potable water, many children died of infections contracted through contaminated water. The polluted beaches, lakes, and lagoons prevented them from being used for leisure activities. A glaring example was Guanabara Bay, which was polluted with sewage, wastes, and industrial pollutants. A four-hundred-million-dollar loan was obtained from the Interamerican Bank to clean and eliminate pollution from the Bay. New jobs were created in this process of cleaning up the pollution, but the major task was to build sewage disposal for the expanding population of Rio.

Another major environmental problem was maintaining the green areas. There were concerns for deforestation, which in many cases was responsible for the mudslides during excessive rainy periods. The development of the *favelas* (slum areas) was essential in the reforesting endeavor. From 1990 through 1994, five hundred acres were reforested in nineteen communities through the concerted effort of the municipal government and the local communities.

Transportation was the third major environmental concern. There were too many cars on the streets, and only a small minority owned these vehicles. Since the car owners were affluent, the government catered to them and invested too much of the financial resources on the roads. The rails were used by only 10 percent of the population, and the vast majority—90 percent—used the buses, which were controlled by the syndicates. Annually, fifty thousand individuals were killed in vehicular accidents in Rio. Transportation in Rio was the main source of air pollution and smog; there was a major fight with bus companies, as there was poor regulation of gas standards. One proposal to curtail the air pollution caused by transportation emphasized the need to develop a bicycle lane network of twelve kilometers (about seven and a half miles), which could provide a means of transportation to work for many *Cariocas* (citizens of Rio de Janeiro).

Since the focus of the Fulbright project was global health and environmental issues, I will further discuss the interrelationship of politics, corruption, environmental, and health issues. First, the federal government provided funds to build housing, obviously for the poor, yet these funds were used to build housing for the rising middle class. Second, on federal government property, illegal builders constructed houses and sold them to the poor. In this land speculation venture, deforestation occurred, and poor people were manipulated. Since these indigent families were living on unsafe, deforested land, where erosion and mudslides occurred, the federal government evicted them for their own protection. A humane approach was needed in removing people and in providing suitable housing to relocate these displaced individuals.

Additional issues in the favelas were crime and drugs. Drug dealers controlled the areas, with the weaponry provided by the profitable, illegal gun trade from the United States. The wealthy Brazilians wanted the army to get involved in the drug-infested areas. The police and politicians took bribes from the drug dealers. The control of the favelas recycled, with the ruling groups getting younger and younger.

Another inexorably intermingled major relationship between environment and health was exemplified by activities at Gramacho, an area where solid waste was dumped, near Guarabara Bay. The poor sought food, salvageable metals, and scrap wood from the waste. Obviously, these individuals came in contact with toxic and other hazardous items. In 1989, the French built two plants for solid waste disposal. The one near the airport operated at 30 percent of its capacity; the other one operated more efficiently, but still there were over six thousand tons of waste dumped daily. The practical solution was to build appropriate waste disposals with modern technology.

Another manner of dealing with the waste problem could be considered a cultural investment. First, people could be encouraged to produce less waste. Second, the schools could teach children recycling techniques. Third, the government could embark upon a venture of buying garbage in the poor areas, thereby creating a healthier environment, while simultaneously providing income for the less fortunate. In sum, this session provided insightful information into the environmental and health concerns of the Brazilian population in Rio de Janeiro.

The remainder of the day was free, so I accepted an invitation from Ben Brothers, a jewelry dealer, to visit his shop in Ipanema. This activity consumed the remainder of the afternoon. I later had dinner alone and retired to my quarters.

SATURDAY, JULY 9, 1994

The day began with a group meeting at nine o'clock. We discussed the modifications in the itinerary. A city tour was planned for three that afternoon but subsequently was canceled. In the late afternoon, I watched a soccer match between Brazil and Holland, since there was

Dr. Thomas O. Edwards

nothing else to do. I gladly joined in the frenzy. Brazil won, and the shops and restaurants reopened as the mass hysteria poured into the streets in great jubilation. As I ate dinner, the conversation at the nearby tables was about ... well, you guessed it—soccer.

SUNDAY, JULY 10, 1994

After breakfast, I participated in a church service with many of the other scholars. It seemed that many missed their Sunday worship. After all, there were two ministers in the group, at least seven choir members, and other churchgoers—even an infrequent one: yours truly. Frank, a young clergyman, held an excellent service. He led the group in hymns, read the scriptures, and delivered a touching sermon about how we need to appreciate and love each other. I truly enjoyed the fellowship, and it helped me create greater solidarity with the group.

In the afternoon I went to the Hippie Market, an open market where artists and artisans brought their wares. Everything could be purchased at this market—leather goods, clothing, and all types of curios. I must have spent at least five hours at the market. I noticed that, quite distinct from my visit five years ago to this same location, merchants and purchasers did not engage in extensive haggling over the prices. I was quite disappointed because this was the aspect of shopping that I enjoyed. I'd get an opportunity to practice my Portuguese and interact with Brazilians during the bartering process. To simply ask the price and pay it was a sterile style of shopping in an open market. When I engaged in extensive dialogue for the items I bought, the items had such a richer value—I could visualize and recreate the scene that took place during the purchase, thereby reliving and cherishing the foreign exchange experience.

In the evening, I didn't follow my better judgment, so I went to a very expensive restaurant with several colleagues. Two of them ordered lobster dinners, which were about seventy dollars each, while I spent around half that amount. Fortunately, I witnessed this type of extravagance only once. I honestly enjoyed the experience, but I doubted that I would do it again.

MONDAY, JULY 11, 1994

We returned to the Igreja e Museu, the Programa Negritude Brasileira (PNB), and were received by the coordinator, Geraldo Rocha. He explained his program on negritude that encompassed five perspectives, several of which were cultural, religious, and popular. The main concern of the program was how to fight racism in a system that denied the existence of racism. After all, Brazil was a "racial democracy." In such a system, blacks survived better psychologically by obscuring their identities. The speaker emphasized that the churches did nothing. Other issues were discussed, such as African American and Latin American theology, ethics, and viewpoints of people who participated in Candomblé.

The behavior expressed in Candomblé is more than religion; African culture and behavior are fermented during the practice of Candomblé. Mr. Rocha informed us of the Museum of Images and Sounds of Rio, where there were pictures that documented the development of the black liberation movement in Brazil. Additionally, this agency had a project with women to determine how discrimination against women could be eliminated. Finally, work in self-discovery occurred in the community. PNB had a significant mission, and there appeared to be major strides toward its realization. The afternoon was free so I did my chores, such as washing clothes and preparing for the next trip.

TUESDAY, JULY 12, 1994

Two major activities occurred. First, there was a trip to the Universidade Do Estado Do Rio de Janeiro, to visit PRAFRO (Programa de Estudos e Debates dos Povos Africanos e Afro-Americanos). This activity was organized by Professor Elisa Larkin Nascimento, the wife of Abdias Do Nascimento. Dr. Flavio Pessoa de Barros, the director of the program housed in the Social Science Center, spoke to us about the function of PROAFRO.

Upon our arrival to the center's office, we saw a host of liberation photographs, posters, and newspaper clippings. Nelson Mandela and Malcolm X were featured on several of these photographic presentations. Dr. Flavio explained the functions of PROAFRO and then discussed Brazilians' general attitudes toward race issues. Dr. Flacio was not African Brazilian, and neither was Professor Larkin Nascimento, even though she was married to Abdias Do Nascimento. I decided I must be viewing things through my African American lens and was unable to understand the complexity of Brazilian race and color issues.

Dr. Flavio stated that Brazil had a special way of dealing with racial issues. Brazil's African Brazilian population was at the bottom of the society, but he said other immigrant groups were at the bottom also. One hundred families manipulated all the wealth of Brazil. Because they carried prejudice toward African Brazilians, others mimicked their behavior. Therefore, discrimination was rooted in cultural identity. Brazil definitely was not a racial democracy. Dr. Flavio developed a dictionary that documented words of African origin that were used in Brazilian Portuguese. The majority of these words had Bantu or Yoruba etymologies. In addition, he wrote about the environment within the practice of Candomblé.

Another major point from the discussion was the role of African Brazilians in society in general. Everyone seemed to recognize the major contributions that this population made in organizing the annual Carnival, but how did these Samba schools benefit economically from their participation in Carnival, beyond winning prizes? That was a question I posed. The response was, "In no other manner." It seemed to me that there was economic exploitation of those who invested all their financial resources and time into participating in Carnival, which was and is a multimillion-dollar industry for Brazil. Another question was, "Has the Samba school organization been used for political purposes?"

There appeared to be a tremendous potential, political and otherwise, in the Samba schools, if channeled appropriately. I could only imagine what would happen if the Samba schools had refused to participate in Carnival—there would not have been a million-dollar business.

Another issue addressed was the polarization of those in the black liberation movement. Some promoted integrating the African Brazilians into a more functioning level within the Brazilian society, while others advocated complete separation. This sounds familiar, doesn't it? A question was raised about how the government policies affected the poor and African population environmentally. The response was that there was very little concern by the government. In 70 percent of the communities of the indigent, there were no sewers or running water. After the discussion with Dr. Flavio, Professor Larkin Nascimento accompanied us as we returned to our van and stated that several of Dr. Flavio's analyses were controversial, so she stated her opinion to us.

"Obviously, it was not appropriate to debate Dr. Flavio during our session, since I served as the translator."

In the afternoon, as the second activity of the day, we went on a brief city tour, highlighted by a visit to Sugar Loaf Mountain. As we traveled there by cable car lift, Rio de Janeiro and the bay were gorgeous to view. At the summit, we photographed a panoramic view of Rio. Next, it was down the mountain and back to the hotel to prepare for the trip to the "jungle."

MANAUS

WEDNESDAY, JULY 13, 1994

We left Rio de Janeiro early in the morning in a canoe on Rio Negro en route to Manaus, the capital of the state of Amazonas. We arrived in Manaus in the late afternoon. After checking in at the hotel and refreshing ourselves, we had a meeting with Mr. Freddie Colon, the secretary of environment for the state. First, he distinguished the

Amazon region from the state of Amazonas. The Amazon region contains 52 percent of Brazil's territory. Within the Amazon are nine Brazilian states; Amazonas is one of them. Many regions of the Amazon are yet to be discovered. The people in the Amazonian state are basically mixed with African, Indian, and European ancestry. The blacks in this area have an extremely small presence, which I witnessed because my individual project involved surveying African Brazilians. I was most cognizant of their lack of physical impact in the city of Manaus. Other issues discussed included the plans to use the abundant fish in the region as an economic base. An industry could be developed, with fish and fish products exported. Health problems identified were malaria and other maladies caused by deforestation. The water from the area needed to be purified for consumption. Developing the culture and environment and improving the education of the people were areas that needed to be considered priorities. Since this appointment was prearranged, we presented Mr. Colon with a plaque, and he was delighted to receive it.

THURSDAY, JULY 14, 1994

I walked to the central shopping district of Manaus after breakfast since there were no scheduled activities until the afternoon. At approximately two o'clock we met at the Secretarira of Saude do Estado do Amazonas and spoke with three representatives, Joaquin De Melo, indolonologist; Leonara Preia, coordinator of health services in Manaus and professor of public health at the University of Amazonas; and Dr. Socrates Moura, statistician. First, we discussed the prevalent diseases in the Amazonas state, which included malaria, typhus, typhoid fever, viruses, bacterial infections, hepatitis, and meningitis. Most of these diseases were a result of the water levels on the river being either too high or too low, and infections were most frequently found in children. Dr. Moura presented some data and indicated that he was developing a data file on health statistics. The main causes of death in 1993 were identified as undefined causes, circulatory problems, external causes, and children's perinatal diseases, such as parasites and respiratory diseases. The infant mortality rate in the city of Manaus and the state of Amazonas was compared; for the state, 48.87, and for the city, 43.96 infant deaths per thousand residents. The number-one cause of death for the women during pregnancy was hypertension. AIDS was not a major problem in this area at that time, since only two deaths from this virus had been reported as of July 1994. Finally, the department collaborated with holistic medicine healers toward improving the general health of the public.

After leaving this seminar, we went to visit the Museu de Cincias Naturias Da Amazonia, where we saw specimens of the various fish, other marine life, insects, and so forth. A splendid collection was on display.

FRIDAY, JULY 15, 1994

Today was a free day, so I used the time to write letters and postcards as well as to prepare for tomorrow's journey to the "jungle," which actually was an ecological reserve. Late in the afternoon we had a meeting to discuss our activities in the rain forest and what clothing and supplies to bring for this three-day journey.

SATURDAY, JULY 16, 1994

At 8:30 a.m., we left the hotel by taxi to go to the docks, where we boarded a boat and traveled down the Rio Negro (Black River). The boat ride was pleasant, lasting about three and a half hours. It became clear why the river is called Rio Negro. The water was very dark, but it looked clean; if you were to scoop a handful, the water would appear clear in your hand. As we left Manaus on the river, we saw floating islands—small land masses. We also saw trees almost totally underwater. Only the very tip of the tree was above water level. The day was sunny and beautiful, so there was no hurry to arrive at our destination. When we arrived at the Terra Verde (Green Land) Village, a tourist resort, we were pleasantly surprised. The facilities consisted of cone-shaped rooms on three levels and bungalows. We had a sumptuous lunch; all the foods were tasty.

Shortly after lunch, the owner and several workers, including the tour guide, Marcos, took us by bus on a jungle expedition through the rain forest. Terra Verde is an ecological reserve owned by Zee, a seventy-two-year-old Polish man, who was a film director. After leaving the bus, we walked through the rain forest, and Marcos lectured us about the various types of trees, plants, fungi, parasites, insects, animals, and all the entities that comprise the ecosystem, as well as their relationships and impact on each other. I experienced an exhilarating feeling of being in harmony with nature. I felt that my inhaling and exhaling air contributed to the maintenance of the rain forest.

When we returned to the lodge, we were treated to a nice dinner. All the food was fresh. After dinner, we were invited to go alligator spotting. Of all the Fulbright scholars, I alone accepted the invitation. I was in a canoe with the tour guide and two locals. With a flashlight, we spotted a caiman. When the flashlight was shone directly in the caimans' eyes, they became immobilized, enabling the holder of the flashlight to approach them. After several attempts to capture the elusive creatures, one of the locals finally snatched one out of the water. It was rather small, about two and a half feet, and its tail had been partially devoured by piranhas. The tail was still bloody. I examined the creature by touching its cold body and had no trepidation at all. This definitely was a baby alligator. Marcos said that it was no more than one and a half years old. I was alligator spotting and could return to tell of my courageous adventure.

It was wonderful being on Rio Negro at night. The stars twinkled so beautifully and a half moon gleamed down from above. It was so peaceful on the river as the frogs and crickets serenaded us. I really cherished those moments—in the middle of Rio Negro at night with a baby caiman in the canoe with me.

Marcos brought the caiman back to the lodge and explained to all the guests who had assembled, including several of the Fulbright scholars. He detailed its age, gender (female), size, and type of life the lost creature experienced. After the lecture and demonstration, the caiman was returned to the river, unscathed by us humans, but it still had to be concerned about the piranhas. I retired to my cone-shaped room on the third floor at ten thirty.

SUNDAY, JULY 17, 1994

At Terra Verde, we met at 6:00 a.m. to take a ride down Rio Negro. Since it was early, the morning was refreshing, and the sun was not too hot. We went into a flooded area off from the river to look for monkeys and other animals. The water level was very high, and we could see some trees completely underwater. After spotting two small monkeys from a distance, we returned to the lodge for breakfast. After breakfast, it was back down the river, searching for monkeys and whatever else we could find. We went through the thicket. One group in another canoe was attacked by bees. Evidently their canoe had disturbed the beehive. For some strange reason, the men in the canoe were stung but the women were untouched.

Later, we were caught in a severe rainstorm while in the canoe. The rain poured so heavily that we could not see in front of us. At least we were out of the thicket and back in the middle of the river, but we were totally drenched. Fortunately, this endured for only about fifteen minutes; then the sun was beaming again. When we arrived at the lodge, those who wanted to disembark did so, but a few others and I wanted more of the river adventure. We were supposedly going to a fishing village. At the village—in reality, another family's place—we saw how the family made its living, including raising common farm animals such as pigs and chickens, farming, and making baskets and other needed items.

We returned to the lodge for lunch. In the afternoon, we—along with all the Brazilians at the lodge—watched the World Cup championship between Italy and Brazil. The pavilion had been arranged for this festivity. Brazil won! The excitement in the jungle paralleled that of Sao Paulo and Rio de Janeiro, except that there were no fireworks or parades down the streets. I imagined if there had been more Brazilians at the lodge, they would have paraded down the river on canoes. Nevertheless, there was a great celebration. I was somewhat annoyed because the entire lodge crew was watching the game, so dinner was not prepared until much later than usual. After dinner, several of the Fulbrighters mustered the courage to go alligator spotting. It wasn't that exciting for me anymore, so I went to bed.

MONDAY, JULY 18, 1994

At the crack of dawn, a small group of us (Alicia, Sylvia, Frank, and staff) jumped into the canoe to go fishing. We caught absolutely nothing. We had breakfast, and almost immediately afterward boarded the boat to return to Manaus. It was a comfortable ride, but I was tired. We stopped for lunch on Rio Negro at a floating restaurant and gift shop that sold mainly Native American artifacts. Later, we continued on Rio Negro until we arrived at a point where the Solimões River met Rio Negro. This is the famous "meeting of the waters." The Solimões River has a yellowish color, and as it commingles with the Rio Negro, the water turns brownish. This union forms the Amazon River. One can clearly see the two colors of the rivers coming together. Just as the rivers come together at a point, they also separate and go in different directions; this phenomenon can be viewed from the opposite perspective. This was a marvelous sight indeed.

I was happy to return to Manaus. Being tired and worn, I ate dinner and retired early.

RECIFE

TUESDAY, JULY 19, 1994

Today was a travel day to Recife, Pernambuco, our fourth city. Hotel departure time was not until noon, so I spent the morning shopping for last-minute souvenirs from Manaus. Our flight time was 2:10 p.m., and after a layover in Brasilia, the capital, we didn't arrive at Recife until eleven thirty that night. The reason for the flight delay was that the victorious soccer team, the World Cup champions (national heroes) had returned to a waiting, jubilant crowd. Their first stop was Recife; therefore, other flights were postponed or delayed. After our arrival, I was excited that we had arrived in a new city that I walked around to explore the immediate area with Willie, another scholar. Our hotel was near the beach, so we went in that direction.

Fulbright Scholars

WEDNESDAY, JULY 20, 1994

The first full day in Recife began with my jogging on the walkway near the beach. I had jogged several times in Rio and Manaus. I was feeling the results of three meals a day from the beginnings of my travels, the buffet breakfasts, all the bread I ate, the beer I drank. After jogging I had breakfast—a plate of fruit, eggs, goat and American cheeses, rolls and buns (you name it; I had it). Then, I drank several glasses of juice and two cups of coffee with milk and sugar.

Later in the morning we had a group meeting that featured a curriculum presentation by Dr. Brenda Burrell, one of the Fulbright scholars. She did an excellent job. Since the focus of our project was curriculum development, she presented an outstanding illustration of how she planned to develop a module in geography utilizing this Fulbright experience. She emphasized that there must be clearly stated objectives, integration of the material into the syllabus of the course, a mechanism for evaluating the implementation, and outcomes. It was obvious that she really had expertise in this area.

After her presentation, we were free for the remainder of the day, except for individual appointments with our group leader, Mr. Oliver Delk. My appointment was 5:00 p.m. In the interim, I went to the laundromat and washed clothes. During the individual meeting, I gave a progress report on my project, and Mr. Delk emphasized the deadline and format of the final project. He also delineated some questions that would be used in evaluating the project, as well as our individual participation in the group. Later in the evening and with the excess energy that I had, I walked from one end of the beach almost to the other, simply observing the people of Recife.

THURSDAY, JULY 21, 1994

Today was our city tour of Recife and visit to Olinda. Several of the highlights were a trip to a Franciscan museum (Casa da Cultura), which was housed in a former jail facility, and visits to a few churches situated on hills in Olinda. After returning from the tour, I decided to take the public bus back downtown to the market. I had seen several items that would be interesting souvenirs, but I didn't have time to purchase them. I also wanted to return to this area because I had seen several African Brazilians, and I wanted to administer my questionnaire to them. After making several small purchases and going to the bank to exchange money, I returned by bus to the hotel

While we were in Brazil, a new currency was introduced, the real. Its purpose was to avert the spiraling inflation that always was prevalent in Brazil. At the same time the United States dollar was at an all-time low against international currencies. As a consequence, the exchange rate varied from R$0.78 to R$0.90 for US $1.00. Imagine getting less Brazilian money for a US dollar! This was a psychologically and financially painful experience.

The remainder of the evening was quiet for me. I had dinner, returned to my quarters, read some material, and retired.

FRIDAY, JULY 22, 1994

We started the morning with a visit to the Federal University of Pernambuco. There, we discussed with several of the professors the condition of the soil and other environmental issues. This seminar was organized by Maria (her surname escapes me), the director of environment for the state of Pernambuco. Two soil analysts (engineers) explained to us how soil could become contaminated from landfills and, as a result, the water sources in the area were jeopardized. Furthermore, poor people were at great risk as they tried to sell material salvaged from the waste at the garbage dumps. Here we could see the interrelatedness of health, environment, and social and economic conditions.

We later visited Professor Herber Campasso, a cartographic and photographmetoric engineer, who explained to us that the green areas being cut resulted in the general area becoming hotter. We next discussed with the chair of the Chemistry Department his research in focusing on the waste products in the production of rum and sugar from cane. Another issue was making greater use of alcohol as fuel for cars.

After the brief seminar at the university, we drove to the environmental secretary's office, where we discussed several concerns with members of her staff. The major environmental problems of Pernambuco were pollution and contamination of water. Marine erosion was getting worse each year, due to artificial docks and the building of houses too close to the beach areas. In addition, there needed to be control of building wells in order to preserve the water supply. Even though 75 percent of the people in the state had running water, safe water still was a priority issue. Deforestation was another environmental concern. It was proposed that a state Council for Environment be developed.

After this discussion, we left to visit the island where the Manatee Center was located. This marine museum also had several aquariums (pools) for the developing and rehabilitating of manatees that were lost or injured. The manatee, often called a sea cow, is a marine mammal. At the time, there was a major campaign in the area to preserve the manatee, hopefully preventing it from becoming extinct.

Later, we had a delicious lunch on the island. The portions of each entrée were so large that we decided to share orders. In the evening, several of us met with two progressive African Brazilians, Veronica and Daniel, who were publishers of an African Brazilian liberation newspaper. We discussed racism, discrimination, and international cooperation toward the development of African consciousness in all people of the diaspora. Veronica spoke fluent English, having learned from her studies in school.

SATURDAY, JULY 23, 1994

In the morning, I met with the Closing Ceremony Committee. We were charged with organizing an ending celebration for the Morehouse College Fulbright Scholars Study Abroad project. We outlined our initial plans for a ceremony to be held on Saturday, July 30, 1994, our final day in Salvador, Bahia. In the early afternoon, I returned to Casa da Cultura, where I administered my survey to a few individuals. I also wanted to make my final purchases in Recife. In the evening, several of us went to a cultural dance show, *Plural Judo e Brasil*, through the invitation of Veronica and Daniel. After the show, Robert, Frank, and I accompanied Veronica to a nightclub, Feititico Tropical. There, we danced, ate, drank, and generally had a good time.

SUNDAY, JULY 24, 1994

The only activity scheduled Sunday was a group meeting at 6:00 p.m. In the late morning, there was parading in the streets. Recife was still celebrating the Brazilian soccer team's winning the World Cup. In the afternoon, Robert, my roommate, and I went to the beach. Francisco, our Brazilian consultant, joined us later. This was true rest and relaxation until the rain came. We sheltered ourselves from the rain until six o'clock, the time of our group meeting. Robert and I, embarrassingly, arrived at the meeting around quarter after six. After the meeting, Robert and I, reflecting on the great time we'd had at Feititico, decided to return and enjoy another evening of fun because our flight on Monday wasn't until 2:30 p.m.

SALVADOR, BAHIA

MONDAY, JULY 25, 1994

We arrived in Salvador, the final city for our project, in the early morning. As always, there was a new burst of energy upon the arrival in a new city. The Tropical Hotel was the most luxurious of the hotels during our stay in Brazil. Several of us decided to go walking to explore the immediate environs. After walking for a while, I convinced Willie to accompany me by bus to the Pelourinho area. Since I had last visited

Salvador five years ago, I was eager to see if there were substantial changes. We took a bus in the general area and arrived at the lower city. In these sections, there was the lower city and the upper city, connected by an elevator and a cable car. We ascended on the elevator and walked around for a while. We stopped at a restaurant in Pelourinho for dinner, walked some more after eating, and then returned to the hotel by taxi.

TUESDAY, JULY 26, 1994

In the morning, we had a city tour of Salvador. I was vaguely familiar with most of the sites. In the afternoon, we visited the office of Olodum, an African cultural organization that initially began as Bloco African Cultural, a group that participated in Carnival. Since then, this group had become socially conscious and was involved in trying to improve the plight of the African Brazilian communities. Olodum used Carnival to protest the conditions in which the population lived. This group was concerned with social, political, and environmental issues.

The music of the group, Olodum, which had become international, resonated with the same consciousness-raising themes. In the evening, we were invited to a musical demonstration by Olodum. The crowd was young and danced to every beat of the drums. Several vocalists also entertained. Tuesdays represent festive activities for the Salvadorans, and there were other musical groups throughout the Pelourinho that evening.

WEDNESDAY, JULY 27, 1994

A morning meeting was canceled, so I went to the Mercado Modelo with several others in the group. We had lunch at SENAC, a well-known restaurant in Salvador; then there was more shopping. It appeared that I bought a lot of items because I frequently shopped, but not all shopping resulted in purchases.

Later that afternoon we met with Dr. Julio Braga, the noted

Brazilian scholar, author, historian, and anthropologist. Dr. Braga was Director of the Center for African and Asian Studies at the Institute of the Federal University of Bahia. ("Asian Studies" is included in the title because, politically, it was not feasible for Bahia, which has an 80 percent African descent population, to have a center for African studies.) Dr. Braga outlined several projects of the Center: an exchange program with Nigeria at the University of Ibadan; the establishment of an African Brazilian museum; and researching original documents that involved the slave trade to Brazil. He also gave a historical analysis of the development of Brazil, the countries from which slaves were brought to Brazil, and the major languages of the slaves. He indicated his political involvement within Bahia. Reading his writings is essential for any serious scholar of Brazilian history and culture.

THURSDAY, JULY 28, 1994

After a breakfast meeting with the Closing Ceremony Committee, we all walked toward downtown, where our seminar would be held at Foundation of the City of Salvador. There, we met Dr. Cid Teixeira, the director of and a professor at the Federal University of Bahia. We discussed the history of Salvador, founded by the British and later colonized by the Portuguese. The Portuguese who came to Salvador were public officials and poor persons seeking a better life. The climate of Brazil was unfavorable to the Europeans, but the African slaves did not have to adapt, since it was the same tropical climate as their origin. We further discussed the thirty-six words used to define or categorize the population of Brazil. Also, Muslims, who came to Brazil around 1835 as slaves were literate, attempted a religious revolution in this predominantly Catholic country. A church constructed with Arabic architecture still stands today, but it is used as a Catholic church. Other enlightening information was that the Spaniards controlled Brazil from 1780 until 1840. This historical discussion with Dr. Teixeria was most informative.

Later, at a group meeting, we discussed the evaluation of the project. Forms were distributed and were to be completed and returned by July 31, 1994.

FRIDAY, JULY 29, 1994

We met in the lobby at nine o'clock to visit the Church of Nosso Senhor do Bonfim (Our Lord of the Good End). This is a famous church on a hill, overlooking the city, where many individuals wearing white clothing attend on Fridays to pray and ask for blessings. Here is where the tradition originated of having a ribbon tied around the left wrist in three knots and making a secret wish as each knot is tied. When the ribbon falls off, then the wishes will come true. As people arrive for the services, young boys tried to tie ribbons on the worshippers' and tourists' wrists and asked for money in the process. There also was a small group of merchants adjacent to the plaza in front of the church. We later drove by an open market and then made a visit to the beach, where young boys were playing soccer. The bus took us to Mercado Modelo, which was our final destination. There, at the market, we had lunch and shopped some more. I used this opportunity to administer my survey.

SATURDAY, JULY 30, 1994

I was counting of the hours before our return to the United States. Ongoing activities were scheduled for the day, but Paula, our tour guide in Salvador, arranged for representatives from the city government's Department of Environment to speak to us at the hotel in the afternoon. Some of the information conveyed was that 75 percent of the population in Salvador did not have a method for disposing sewage; sanitation was a major problem; and beaches were polluted in the center of the city, although most of Bahia still had beautiful beaches. In the favelas, solid waste and toxic materials were pollution concerns for the inhabitants. Children were dying in these favelas as a result of the unsanitary conditions. Because of the lack of housing in the city, people built houses wherever they could, but no city services were provided. Bus transportation created some degree of air pollution, but Salvador was fortunate in that it received constant breezes from the ocean, thereby generally resulting in clean air.

Other information that was given centered around groups that were formed to deal with the environment. The Council for the Protection of the Environment was formed in 1972, and after the Rio 1992 conference, other similar groups were formed. Olodum, as mentioned earlier, was involved with environmental protection. Candomblé, the African-based religion, was a forerunner of protection for the environment because leaves are sacred and are used in many aspects of the religion. Augusto Saraiva Piexato and Verna Fariais, representatives from the Group for Environmental Recomposition, also spoke, noting that only half of the eight thousand tons of trash is collected per day. A particular environmental and human hazard is the favela Alagados, which is situated on a river. Infants die from accidental drowning, and young children succumb to infectious diseases from contaminated water. These environmental and health problems primarily affected the poor and disenfranchised, so the government did not deem the issues worthy of financial investment.

At around five o'clock we met for our group picture and the closing ceremony. We had a lovely program. All the Fulbright scholars had an opportunity to participate, either by singing, praying, or presenting. All the participants were given personalized key chains with the individual's name carved in wood. The groups' leaders and consultants were given individual plaques. We had a scrumptious meal, and the activities ended joyously, with all of us in a circle of unity, wishing for the continuation of the friendship and professional collaboration. Even though this was Saturday night, not too many of us were interested in hanging out on our final night in Salvador. We wanted to pack and be ready for the 5:30 a.m. departure from the hotel and return trip to Rio, then to Sao Paulo, and, finally, to Atlanta, Georgia.

SUNDAY, JULY 31, 1994

We arrived in Rio de Janeiro at approximately 10:10 a.m. Our flight from Rio to Sao Paulo was scheduled to depart at nine o'clock that night. Even though we were anxious to return home, we wondered what to do with so much time. I decided to go into Rio with Robert and Francisco to the Hippie Market, simply to kill time. We took a bus from the airport and arrived at the market area around one o'clock. We ventured off in our individual directions, agreeing to meet at three o'clock to return to the airport. When it was time to return, however, we had difficulty finding the bus stop for the correct bus. We boarded a bus going to the airport—the local airport, *not* the international airport from which we were scheduled to depart. Of course, the two airports were in opposite directions. We worried about getting to the international airport, but an even greater problem was our Brazilian financial situation. None of us had that many reais (*reais* is the plural of real). We'd been trying to spend them so we wouldn't return to the United States with any, except a few for souvenir purposes. We counted what we collectively had to determine if we had a sufficient amount for taxi fare. We had about thirteen reais and taxi fare was estimated at thirteen to fourteen reais or more. We negotiated with a taxi driver who agreed to take us. The fare was ten reais. As far as I was concerned, he could keep every real that I had. Since I lost so much money in the currency exchange, I really didn't care to see reais at all.

When it was time to board the plane, I was just as anxious as those who had been counting the hours, three days earlier. Even though I enjoyed every week, day, hour, minute, and second in Brazil, I was now ready to go home. I knew that when we arrived in Atlanta at ten in the morning, I still would have to make the journey to New York. I would not get home until seven o'clock that night, some nine hours after landing on US soil.

The Brazilian Fulbright scholar experience was fantastic. My previous visits to Brazil in 1988 and 1989 did not compare to the educational enlightenment, professional development, and personal growth that I experienced from June 24 to July 31, 1994.

INDIVIDUAL PROJECT

"Psychological Health of African Brazilians as It Relates to Identity"

Consistent with the theme of the Fulbright Study Abroad program, which was "Global Health and Environmental Issues: An Interracial Survival Imperative—Focusing on Brazil," I examined issues related to the psychological health of African Brazilians, especially their sense of identity. I contend that one's sense of identity is directly related to one's ability to have a global or local perspective. That is, if one views oneself as a Brazilian or as a resident of an individual state, then one's perspective is limited, whereas if one views oneself as an African Brazilian, then that perspective is more expansive, connecting one to Africa and the African diaspora. In other words, in developing a global perspective, which is essential in today's technologically advanced world, one must begin with an identity that fosters a nexus with all persons who share a common ancestry. In sum, for one to be concerned with global and environmental issues, one, first of all, must become a part of that "global village" and then commit oneself to improving it and eliminating its deleterious conditions.

In Brazil, I collected information from African Brazilians of all social, educational, and economic classes. I was particularly interested in how both professionals and laypersons classified themselves in reference to their heritage. (For example. Were there African roots, indigenous roots, European roots?) To what extent did African Brazilians cherish each aspect of their heritage? How did this identity relate to a globalized or international focus?

Since we traveled to five different cities in five different states, I attempted to collect data from each locale. In identifying African Brazilians, I selected for my sample only those persons who had distinct Negroid features, such as skin color, texture of hair, and facial characteristics. I administered a questionnaire consisting of six items to thirty-five African Brazilians—four from Sao Paulo, eight from Rio de Janeiro, one from Manaus, seven from Recife, and fifteen from Salvador. The questionnaire requested the respondents to indicate the following: (1) "How do you identify yourself? As an African Brazilian, Brazilian, or member of an individual state (Paulista, Biano, etc.)." (2) "How old are you?" There were five categories, such as 18–25, 26–34, etc. (3) "What is your highest level of education (elementary school, high school, college, graduate school, specialized study)?" (4) "What is your sex?" (5) "Do you think that Brazilians should want to visit Africa?" (6) "Does Brazil have many problems with pollution?" To these two final questions, the response choices were yes or no.

To the first item, self-identification,

- 9 persons identified themselves as African Brazilian
- 14 selected Brazilian
- 12 related to their individual state as their focus of identity

In the second item, age group,

- 10 were between the ages of 18 and 25
- 9 respondents each were in the 26–34 and the 35–43 categories
- 6 were between 44 and 50
- 1 was over 50

The third item, sampling education, yielded the following:

- 18 had attended elementary school
- 7 completed high school
- 5 were college graduates
- 2 had graduate school education
- 3 had specialized beyond graduate school

There were fifteen females and twenty males in the sample. All the respondents agreed that Brazilians should want to visit Africa and that Brazil had many problems with pollution.

In sum, some general observations can be made from the above. Of the thirty-five respondents, over half of them—eighteen—had attained only an elementary education. Only nine self-identified as African Brazilian; of these, seven had college or advanced degrees. Being Brazilian was selected by fourteen respondents, and identification with one's state was chosen by twelve respondents. The vast majority of identification with one's state was indicated by respondents who had only attended elementary school, ten of twelve.

In this report, I, through a pilot study, investigated the psychological health of African Brazilians by examining their sense of identity. Most did not self-identity as African Brazilians. The greatest number (fourteen) self-identified as Brazilian, and the second highest number (twelve) identified themselves as members of their individual states. One can conclude that nearly three-fourths of the sample had a more localized perspective of their sense of identity. The explanations for refusing to self-identify as African Brazilian were several: the miscegenation within Brazilian society; possible denial due to negative portrayal of Africans in general; and a lack of formal education. Perhaps there are other dynamics in the Brazilian society that would more adequately account for the African Brazilians' patterns of self-identification, but these were undetected in this brief and limited study. Obviously, this topic seems to have promising prospects for future research into the nuances and subtleties of Brazilian society, generally, and African Brazilians, specifically.

CURRICULUM DEVELOPMENT MODULE

Cross-Cultural Psychology

Since curriculum development is the major thrust of the Fulbright Scholars Study Abroad program, I have revised the syllabus of one of my courses that has a global/international focus. As a professor of a cross-cultural psychology course, participation in this project has enabled me to enrich my instruction by integrating my own experiences and research in Brazil into my lectures. Furthermore, from the resources that I have acquired, I can now assign additional readings for my students so they will be able to appreciate more fully the Brazilian population. With this background, my students will be able to understand realistic examples of cross-cultural psychological functioning by comparing Brazilians and Americans, particularly those of African descent from each country. The specific attention to Brazil will improve students' interest and engender other comparative endeavors.

The syllabus for the cross-cultural psychology course, PSYC 326, is revised as follows: in addition to the present course objectives, the following will be added. "To compare and contrast the psychological functioning of African Brazilians and African Americans." Moreover, "Students will analyze the similarities and differences in self-identification of African Brazilians and African Americans." Additional readings of books by Brazilian authors, recent articles from psychological journals, and video presentations about the Fulbright Scholars Study Abroad program also will be utilized. Students will be evaluated with this Brazilian component by their submitting a typewritten paper, comparing and contrasting a chosen aspect of African Brazilian and African American psychological functioning.

CHAPTER 8

SAFARI INSTRUCTOR TO KENYA, AUGUST 1995

M s. Dorothy Dunson, a tour organizer, asked me to accompany a group of individuals who were going to Kenya on a safari. My role was to serve as a lecturer who would provide historical and cultural information in the context of the travel. In addition to Ms. Dunson and me, the group consisted of a writer for television shows; his wife, Patty; their twelve-year-old son; Delores, a teacher from the Bronx, New York; Gloria, a nineteen-year-old woman who had emotional problems; her mother; and her stepfather. As we were on our final flight from London to Kenya, having arrived in England from John F. Kennedy International Airport in New York, we encountered Ms. Jane Goodall, the world-renown anthropologist and expert on chimpanzees, who was on board.

When we arrived in Kenya, we were greeted by Mr. Limo Kollum, a former consul general for the Kenyan Consulate in California. He would serve as our local guide. In Nairobi, we lodged at the Kenya Safari Club, where we could see wild animals coming to a water hole to drink and bath. This was our first glimpse of the exquisite animals that would enrich our visits to Kenya and Tanzania.

One of the first excursions was a visit to a Maasai village. The Maasai tribe is an extremely astute and savvy group. You may remember them from their participation in American Express commercials several years ago. They are, on average, tall and slender but healthy. They wear their traditional garb, lightly clad, and carry spears. From their appearance you might conclude that they are unsophisticated, but they are just the opposite. The Maasai are adept in exploiting the tourists; for example, they expect you to pay them to take a photograph of them or with them. They will dance for a fee, but dancing, for them, means simply jumping in place, higher and higher. They raise cattle, and cows are their major commercial exchange. Cow dung is used to build their huts, but the odor does not remain with the structure. During our interactions with the Maasai, one of the young men of the village became enamored with Gloria, who was overly friendly with the males. He spoke to his father about this, and his father wanted to know who Gloria's father was because he wanted to make an offer for marriage on behalf of his son—fifty cows for the young lady. Obviously, the negotiation failed, and Gloria continued to travel with us.

We also visited the Kambi Garba School, an institution for children whose parents are primarily nomads. Several individuals from the United States who had been on previous safaris with Ms. Dunson had "adopted" this school and agreed to support it. On behalf of those persons as well as the rest of us, we delivered numerous school supplies for the children, and they were exceedingly joyous and grateful to receive them. The children, in return, had made very nice containers from indigenous gourds to send to their benefactors. It was a wonderful experience to converse with the dedicated teachers and staff, as well as to see the beautiful smiles of the well-cared-for children.

The most significant aspect of the safari was the time visiting the Maasai Mara National Reserve, which is contiguous with the Serengeti Plains in Northern Tanzania. There, we saw the migration of thousands and thousands of wildebeests, zebra, and Thomson gazelles, crossing the vast expanse. Simultaneously, lions, leopards, cheetahs, and other predators realized that dinner was plentiful whenever hunger arose. It should be noted that these wildcats only killed their prey when they were hungry and not for sport or animosity. During one of these occasions, I captured on film the complete scene of a lioness, tracking, tackling, and beginning to devour a wildebeest. The photographing of this episode was so beautiful that it could have been shown on *National Geographic* programs. I was so proud of my professional shooting that I constantly rewound the film to marvel at my fantastic skills. Then, shortly afterward, when we had arrived from the day's excursion, I saw several baboons engaging in play activities in front of the lodge, and my camera began to roll again, not realizing that I did not forward wind my captivating lioness-overpowering-the-wildebeest scene. What a major frustrating disappointment! Other animals with which we had close encounters were elephants, giraffes, rhinos, buffalos, and warthogs. We were even able to see scavengers such as vultures come for the clean-up.

While we stayed at the Mount Kenya Safari Club, made famous by the legendary film star William Holden, we experienced a very special evening. I felt that this extravaganza was equivalent to Captain's Night on a cruise ship. At this exotic lodge, with very comfortable bungalows and beautifully manicured lawns, we had an exciting party with a six-course meal. We were required to dress in no less than semi-formal attire. I wore an elegant green double-breasted suit with matching tie and handkerchief. We were entertained by Kenyan drummers and traditional dancers. Champagne was available for purchase at approximately fifty dollars per bottle. Since it was an evening of decadence, I didn't deny myself or the guests in my company.

In Kenya, we enjoyed the beauty of the beach at the Mombasa Beach Hotel. At Lake Nakuru, it was wonderful to see pink flamingoes and white rhinos. As most people think of Africa as being a warm or hot continent, it was marvelous to see the snow-capped mountains of Kilimanjaro.

Dr. Thomas O. Edwards at the Mount Kenya Safari Lodge.

Prof. Edwards in slave chamber on the coast of Zanzibar.

Mohammed in Zanzibar sitting on the giant turtle.

Toward the end of the official safari, the clients were escorted back to Nairobi by Ms. Dunson, the coordinator, while Delores, the teacher and the other African American on the safari, and I traveled to Zanzibar, where Ms. Dunson would meet us in a few days. In Zanzibar, we met a car driver, Mohammed, who served as our host and guide. He showed us the historic sites, including a spice farm. Then we saw a gigantic turtle that was about two feet high and four feet long. Mohammed sat on the turtle without causing any harm to it. Next, we saw a Muslim museum that had photographs of omans, who had been rulers in the area. Another site was the ruins of a palace of the third oman, the Arab ruler of Zanzibar. A partial section of what had been the bathing area for the women in the oman's harem still remained. What intrigued me the most was a "slave chamber," as it was called, near the ocean, which was the holding cell for those captured, who then would be sold to the merchants arriving by ship. This slave hole was rather small and hidden among some natural rocks. When I climbed down into it, I could barely stand, and there was very little room to maneuver. This slave chamber was smaller in size than the slave dungeon ("castle") of Senegal, and they both demonstrated a lack of regard for human dignity.

Otherwise, Zanzibar is an exquisite and extraordinarily beautiful island. I will always remember the gorgeous sunset on the Indian Ocean as evening approached. Such a wonderful sight enriches the spirit, and the feelings that glow within are indescribable. Experience from traveling provides a unique education that is gratifying and difficult to communicate due to the individual's intrinsic, personal, emotional, and harmonious interactions with the environment at that point in time. Certain affective involvements with nature can't be conceptualized or communicated intellectually.

After enjoying the beach in Stone Town on Saturday, we boarded a ferry that took us back to Dar Es Salam, Tanzania, where we spent the day on Sunday. Then it was back to Nairobi, where we boarded our flight to JFK International Airport in New York.

CHAPTER 9

FACULTY LIAISON—
CUNY STUDY ABROAD PROGRAM

SUMMER 1997 IN TANZANIA

C UNY Study Abroad offers students a wide range of short-term, semester, and year-long programs that lead to significant cultural and academic experiences. I agreed to supervise two male students, Ronnie and Aknaktum, who majored in social sciences, with their approved projects, which would be conducted within a small community in Tanzania, Mbeya.

FRIDAY, JULY 18, 1997

After a long, arduous journey, we arrived in Dar Es Salam at approximately 11:00 p.m., local time. The travel from JFK Airport commenced 7:30 p.m. eastern daylight time. There was a delayed layover in Amsterdam, Holland, and a forty-minute stop in Kilimanjaro. With a six-hour time difference, our bodies experienced serious jet lag. However, since we were served a snack, dinner, and breakfast on the flight, we had the energy to make the adjustment once we were in Dar Es Salam. The transition through immigration and customs was smooth, but we could not connect with our host. Therefore, we took a taxi to the local Continental Hotel, where the accommodations were modest but comfortable. My room had an operating fan and a noisy air conditioner, but who was I to complain? *Lala Salama Good Night/ Sleep Well).*

SATURDAY, JULY 19, 1997 (HAPPY BIRTHDAY, BROTHER GREG)

I slept well at night. I met with the students the next morning for breakfast. Then we walked through the town, seeking a post office, as we'd been informed that we could make calls to the States from there, and we all wanted to inform our families of our safe arrival. As we walked the streets, we met a gentleman who took us to the post office, but we discovered we needed a phone card to make international calls—or we could go to the brand-new post office to make the calls.

Before looking for the new post office, I made a local call to Mr. Richard Chengula, the liaison (host), who hadn't met us when we arrived at the airport. He didn't answer his phone, but I left a message that we were in town. As we looked for the new post office, we found a place where international calls could be made. We all called home, 9:30 a.m. Tanzanian time but 3:30 a.m. New York time. We also faxed a note to David Robinson, son of the legendary baseball player Jackie Robinson. David would be accommodating us at his home as we engaged in the assigned projects. After walking about for a while, we returned to the hotel at eleven thirty.

I rested for a couple of hours, had lunch (king fish and rice), and then went for a walk in the opposite direction from the hotel. I saw many vendors in the streets trying to sell all types of wares: artifacts, clothing, food, and so on. Since it was rather hot in the early afternoon, I decided not to walk too long, but it was long enough that I was perspiring profusely. Upon returning to my room, I tried to watch television. The reception was very poor, but there was a rerun of the television series *Amen*, which I enjoyed. When that program ended, wrestling was the programming—on both channels. I decided that studying Kiswahili was a more fruitful activity. Then I took a rather long nap for the afternoon. Later, I went to the outside restaurant to relax and have a beer. As I sat alone, several "ladies" tried to get my attention, but I was just staring into space. Finally, one came over, started a conversation, and propositioned me, but I would have nothing to do with her, except to be friendly and try to learn some Kiswahili words; however, she spoke English rather well.

Later, Aknaktum, the birthday boy, came down, and after he had his meal, we joined some of the "ladies" for conversation, even though they had other agendas. Neither of us was going to fall into the trap. Another woman joined the group, and she appeared to be cosmopolitan. We learned she had traveled all over Europe. Her English was flawless. We talked with her about America, the other ladies, white people, and all sorts of other things. Finally, we parted company, and off to bed I went.

SUNDAY, JULY 20, 1997

I awoke in the morning at six o'clock, bathed, washed clothes, and then I searched for the students at around seven thirty so that we could take our journey to Zanzibar. They, however, were still in bed and indicated that it would be better if we visited Zanzibar when we returned from Bara, where Mbeya is located. Since it was early, I decided to take a walk, starting in the direction of the airport but then detouring. As I walked along the streets, I saw many buses, and people were selling items—from biscuits to batteries and everything in between. I was surprised that I didn't get lost because I walked in a complete circle. When I returned, I had breakfast—Spanish omelet, bread, and tea. After purchasing some water, I returned to my room and experienced the electricity being off for the first time; therefore, neither my ceiling fan nor the noisy air conditioner would operate.

Surprisingly, it wasn't too hot then, around 9:45 a.m. By 12:40 p.m., however, I was getting very hot, so I left the room to sit in the outside lobby area, studying Kiswahili while I waited for my two students. We were invited by a hotel guest to visit her "grocery" (restaurant), located outside of town. At three o'clock a prearranged driver took Ronnie and me to her place. (Aknaktum didn't feel up to going.) There, we conversed and drank beer. Later, we were treated to a delicious meal of fish cooked with vegetables, peas, carrots, plantains, and other local delicacies. It was really wonderful being away from the center of town and interacting with local people. At around seven thirty, we left to return to the hotel. Back at the hotel, we sat and talked some more, especially about the diva's (cosmopolitan lady's) desire to come to the States to sell rubies and other precious gemstones. Somewhere around eleven thirty, I was off to bed.

MONDAY, JULY 21, 1997

I was up at 6:40 and prepared to go to Mbeya by train. (This was the site where the project was to be completed.) At around eight o'clock, Ronnie and I started walking, looking for a locale where we could exchange money. As we walked along the streets, there was a lot of hustle and bustle, typical of any urban environment. We also stopped to buy stamps and envelopes. When we returned, I finally got through to Mr. Chengula, our contact (supposedly). He met us at the hotel, but he didn't know anything about us or our trip to Mbeya. Neither did he think that David Robinson knew about our arrival because they had spoken a week ago, and there was no mention of us. However, Mr. Chengula did assist us in arranging for a bus to Bosic, and from there we could hire a car to Bara. He was very nice to us and offered to pick us up at six o'clock to have some beer.

I expected the bus experience to be an interesting one. We were scheduled to leave at 5:30 a.m., arrive in Bosic at 2:00 p.m., and then take a car to Bara for an evening arrival. I hoped that David Robinson would be home and that he wouldn't be too surprised. There was no way to contact him in advance to announce our arrival. I was looking forward to this safari; I was very open-minded and prepared for whatever happened. I decided to just sit back and enjoy the rest of the day in Dar.

At around one thirty, after a short rest, I called Mr. Chengula and agreed to meet him to exchange dollars to shingili. His office was only a few blocks from the hotel. It was nicely paneled, had a carpet, and displayed a new quiet air conditioner. I had tea with him and transacted our business. He arranged a better exchange rate than we had received earlier, even though he took a commission of five shingili per dollar. When I left his office, I went to the Rendezvous Restaurant, which ended up being a trip in and of itself. I ordered fried fish fillet. When I took a bite, I thought it tasted like chicken. During this time, I was eating only seafood and no other meats. When I insisted that it was chicken, the waiter politely maintained that it was fish. I smelled it and asked him to smell it, and I was adamant about it not being fish. The waiter politely took it away. This disagreement was conducted respectfully on both ends. Later, the owner came to apologize, stating that perhaps it tasted like chicken because it had been fried in batter. He had another piece prepared but cooked differently. It had the same texture but a very faint aroma of fish. I knew that this piece was the same as the first, so I realized this fish was unfamiliar. There are many exotic types of fish in various locales. Some are very fleshy and quite different from the fish in the United States. I ate it, and it was satisfactory. I told the waiter that I was sorry and that the fish was good, and it was my first time having it. I returned to the hotel and took a short rest. Before I knew it, Mr. Chengula was there to take us out.

He had a very nice van, similar to a Voyager. His wife was with him, and he took us to one of his fresco-style restaurants. We sat there for a while and had refreshments. Later, we went to his second restaurant, which was much larger. A very big, lively crowd was assembled. We had more refreshments, and then he brought us back to the hotel around eleven o'clock.

As we walked into the hotel, we were approached by Pilly, the lady who had invited us to lunch the day before. She wanted us to have some beer with her before we retired. As we sat talking, we noticed another group of ladies, one of whom Aknaktum had met the night before. When she was left alone, we invited her to our area. Why did we do that? A fierce argument erupted between the two women, speaking in Kiswahili. Several men of Asian descent were enjoying the ruckus as they were brought into the melee as arbiters. This dispute lasted a long while. By the time it ended and we left to go to bed, it was quarter to three. We had planned to awake at four o'clock to meet the bus to Mbeya by five o'clock. I didn't go to bed; I simply repacked my things for the all-day bus ride.

TUESDAY, JULY 22, 1997

Tuesday seemed like a continuation of Monday since I didn't get any sleep. The bus departed at 5:40 a.m., as vendors surrounded the bus for final sales. I bought a big loaf of unsliced bread. The trip started out fine, and the bus, with primarily male passengers, was not very crowded. The bus' destination was Lusaka, Zambia. The road was in excellent condition, and the driver behaved as if he were on the Indianapolis Motor Speedway, even when he was negotiating sharp contours high in the mountains. We made one pit stop, for lunch and a bathroom break. Ronnie purchased an interesting dish, a potato omelet of sorts—soft-fried potatoes mixed with eggs. However, I enjoyed baked red fish with a side of potatoes. I tried sleeping as much as possible during the journey until the 4:00 p.m. arrival in Mbeya.

When we disembarked, we inquired for David Robinson. No one understood us initially, but one young man finally said, "Mr. Robinson," and then others understood. We looked a sight—all that luggage and not knowing where we were going. We hired a taxi driver who took us to a friend of Mr. Robinson. It turned out that this friend lived directly behind the bus station. Mr. Omar Shariff was very nice. He invited us to his lovely house and stated that we could leave our luggage there overnight, while we took the things we needed to spend the night in a rooming house. The journey to Mr. Robinson's place would take several hours so we couldn't start the journey until the next morning. As we walked to the rooming house, guided by a young man, we were called back dramatically. Mr. Robinson was in town, and were we happy to see him! We introduced ourselves and, of course, he didn't know that we were coming at that time. Mr. Robinson indicated that he had spoken to Michael Hooper, the United States liaison for the project, back in March, but nothing was confirmed in terms of dates and time.

We made the journey to Bara with Mr. Robinson, first taking transportation to Mlowo. From there we had to transfer to another vehicle to take us to Itaka. Mr. Robinson had left his jeep at Itaka, so we rode with him to his farm. It was a long ride on an unpaved road. We eventually arrived around 9:30 p.m. I was exhausted.

When we retired in a concrete house, we saw there were no beds, only two straw mats and a foam mattress David Robinson had purchased. Ronnie and I took the mats, while Aknaktum used the mattress. Ronnie had a sleeping bag, but I didn't. I slept on the cold, concrete floor with only a thin half sheet and my robe on top of me. I was cold all night, but I did sleep in spurts.

WEDNESDAY, JULY 23, 1997

I woke up around quarter to seven and was happy to get up off the cold floor. It had to be warmer outside. I ate some bananas that had been purchased the night before and later drank tea and ate bread. By eight thirty I was ready for my full day in Bara. Mr. Robinson had to go into the village, so we decided to take it easy and acclimate ourselves to the environs.

David Robinson owned a coffee farm. I walked through it and observed the coffee trees. In one section men were harvesting the crops, picking the beans from the trees. Later, we received some warm and cold water to prepare for our baths. There was a bathroom, literally a stall for bathing. The toilet was a couple of doors down. The toilet, a latrine type, had the fixture (commode) on the floor, and we had to squat over it to use it. When you have to go, you have to go! It really wasn't that bad.

For the rest of the day we lounged around and played with David's six-year-old twin daughters, Rachel and Laura. They received schooling from a teacher who came to the house from 8:00 a.m. until 1:00 p.m. After lunch, I took a brief nap and studied more Kiswahili. In the afternoon, upon David's return, we discussed the details of the project, including a tentative plan for its completion. We had dinner, more of the same as lunch—rice with peas and cabbage. We ate African style, all from the same platter, but somewhat modified because we had spoons. After dinner, I took a short walk to the warehouse and back. The warehouse where the coffee beans were stored was guarded because there had been a previous robbery. David spent the night in the warehouse with another worker, and both were armed. Later that evening, we moved to another room that had a door. Even though the other rooms had defined dimensions, there were only open spaces between them. We were given a shotgun for protection. The night was peaceful. *Lala Salama!(Good Night/ Sleep Well)*

THURSDAY, JULY 24, 1997

After a hurried breakfast, we were on our way to the Bara village. Stanley drove us there to meet the chairman and other officials. First, however, we stopped by David's son, Howard's, shop; he was the one who would take us around. The chairman was there, but it was the vice chairman who received us. We signed the guest book. Then we went to the school site, and I discovered that we were not going to build a secondary school; instead, our project was to complete a library that had been under construction but was abandoned. The vice principal escorted us around to meet all the classes. The older children, third grade to seventh grade, studied English as a subject. All the other instructions were in Kiswahili. The older children greeted us in English after they were instructed to do so. They politely stood when the vice principal entered the room. When he asked them to be seated, they all repeated in unison, "We are sitting down." The younger children only spoke Kiswahili and their native African language.

Later, we did meet the chairman. Other men of the village were present also. We were now formally registered as guests of the village, and Howard explained our purpose for being there. We then went to the project site and saw what had to be done. We agreed that the school children would bring the brick from the kiln to the building site. Afterward, we returned to Howard's shop and house, where his wife had prepared lunch for us—ugali(cornmeal cooked with water to a dough-like consistency) with dried fish, cooked in peanut oil. I enjoyed the meal. Shortly after lunch we started on our safari, walking back to David's house, which was about four to five miles. We started at 4:00 and arrived at 5:40. It was an exhausting walk because there was nothing except hills and dust. We were all extremely tired. Aknaktum went straight to sleep and did not get up to take a bath or to have dinner when it was prepared. He got up later, long after we had finished, looking for his meal. After the bath, dinner, and a gaze at the beautiful stars, I was ready for bed. I tried to study some Kiswahili, but my eyes had different ideas. I was asleep at around nine o'clock.

FRIDAY, JULY 25, 1997

I woke up around two in the morning because I had gone to bed so early. I tried to remain in bed, even though I had an urgent need to urinate. Finally, I got up and went outside to relieve myself. When I returned to bed, I still could not sleep. All I could hear were animals outside or inside, making noises. It sounded as if they were fighting, but it was probably raccoons trying to get water from the pails. The noise was so loud that I thought it had to be inside. I mustered up enough bravado to get up with my flashlight to see if the animals were actually inside. They were not. I went back to bed, and, as I thought about all my family and friends, I went back to sleep.

I got up around seven thirty and dressed in my work clothes. We had our usual tea and *mandazi*, or baked bread. David drove us to town, we met Howard, and we all went to the job site. The children had brought some bricks. We expected other townspeople, who were going to help, would be there, but no one was there. We were eager to get started, so we agreed to organize the bricks. First, we removed the old bricks that had been left around the unfinished structure when the project had begun. Then we organized the new bricks. Some were broken already, and as we moved others, more broke. It was hot, but we kept working. Later, Howard returned with shovels that looked as if they were turned inside out; they looked more like hoes, but as we got accustomed to them, they worked. By around 12:50 p.m., we decided to stop. We had labored for less than two hours, but we had started, and that's what was important.

We went to Howard's and waited for lunch, which consisted of rice, beans, and chicken in a savory sauce. The meal was most gratifying. We then waited for the jeep, which was going to take us to the local fair. All the townsfolk, dressed in their best clothing, were going there. Howard's wife and daughter went along with David's daughters and the house worker. Lots of people were buying used Western clothing, African print materials, and all other sorts of local products. Food and drinks were also sold. Ronnie bought fabric and flip-flops, and Stanley and I had a beverage. Everyone was about business, buying what was needed and departing. I noticed that as most people left, they were eating a small stick of sugar cane. We returned from the fair late in the evening. I wrote my journal entry at 8:15 while waiting for dinner, which wasn't ready because the entire household had been at the fair, including the cook.

After dinner, it was straight to bed at ten o'clock. Sleeping was an adventure in itself. Even though I went to bed at ten, by two in the morning I was wide awake. I wondered what I should do when there were no lights and no privacy—I shared the large room with my two students. Here I lay there in the middle of the night with severe gas, yet I couldn't expel a serious flatulence. So I lay there, allowing it to seep out slowly. After about an hour I got up, went outside, and genuinely farted. When I returned, I lay there again, wide awake, thinking about being home in my own bed and asking myself, "Why am I as I am?" and "What do I want to do in the near future?" I even thought about work. Somewhere after 4:30 a.m. I fell asleep, but the wake-up call was around 6:00 a.m.

SATURDAY, JULY 26, 1997

After our tea and mandazi, we headed to the village to begin a half day of work. As David was driving us, we ran out of gas, but he had picked up a supply on the way. Once he put the gas in the tank, with my assistance, he opened the hood so that he could get it to flow to the carburetor. As he sucked the hose and touched a wire, the car started and moved backward down a hill. Since Ronnie, Aknaktum, and another passenger were inside, I tried to stop the jeep but to no avail. David jumped into the vehicle and tried to control it, but it moved farther down the hill. Finally, he had it under control.

We arrived at the work site, gathered the tools we needed, and began to clean the inside of the structure, preparing for the foundation. We hoed, shoveled, and pick-axed. We removed many rocks and got half of it done. Later, the mason came so we mixed cement with the sand that was there. There was cooperation from the village as some women brought water, and several men helped with the other construction work. We worked until one o'clock, accomplishing quite a bit. As usual, we went to Howard's for lunch and then returned to the farm. I was so tired that I took off the work clothes, put on some shorts, and took a nap. I got up, started studying Kiswahili, and wrote in my journal. It got dark around seven thirty.

SUNDAY, JULY 27, 1997

The tea and mandazi were on the table, waiting for us when we went to breakfast. Ronnie was already at the table when I joined him at 11:20. I had some chai and mandazi; then I studied my Kiswahili-English book for a while. I cleaned out a candle dish, one from Ronnie, so that I could use it to cleanse my dentures. I thought about washing some clothes but after realizing how scarce the water was, I changed my mind. I decided that this was a good time to repair my black leather bag from Brazil. The strap was broken from all the man-handling during travel. I had some Super Glue that I had purchased in Dar to repair my sandals and the heels on one of my soft shoes, also purchased in Brazil. The glue, however, was dried out and useless. Then I remembered I had brought a sewing kit. I worked on the bag for a couple of hours while listening to the music of Toni Braxton and a few other tapes—David had electricity supplied by solar energy. It worked well but was limited.

I had wanted to use this Sunday as a time of reflection, but I'd had several activities already, and I also wanted to write some letters so that they would be ready for posting on Tuesday when David went into Mbeya. I imagined my reflections would have to wait until later. In the afternoon, I rested until dinnertime, but we had to wait for dinner since the cook and the rest of the family were in the village. I remembered that I'd brought six cans of tuna, and I thought this was the time to open several of them. The other guys said they didn't eat tuna, so I grabbed one can and tried to open it with my pocket knife. I didn't make much progress, but I found a knife in the kitchen that did the job. I enjoyed the tuna and later studied Kiswahili. Finally, the family arrived, and dinner was prepared. We ate, and I went to bed around nine thirty.

MONDAY, JULY 28, 1997

At 1:40 a.m., I was wide awake. I did my usual tossing and turning . I started thinking about everything, everybody, and even work—for example, who would teach the classes and who should not return as adjuncts? I got up to urinate but remained outside to marvel at the stars. It's hard to imagine the beauty of being high on the mountain, with nothing between you and the stars except the sky. Finally, at 6:40 a.m., I was up out of bed, preparing for another day of work. David drove us in at around 7:50, and we arrived at the village, assembled the equipment, and went to work. We picked the other side of the structure to prepare for the foundation. Then it was mixing cement and assisting the masons (*fundis*) in laying bricks for the opposite side of the construction, beginning at the two corners and working our way to the center. We finished around one o'clock and then went to Howard's house and waited for lunch, which wasn't ready until three thirty. Ronnie and I walked back to the farm, talking about Medgar Evers, primarily. Aknaktum waited in the village for David to return from Itaka. Later, it was a bath and dinner around quarter after eight. Dinner was rice, beans, cabbage with carrots, and greens. It appeared I was becoming a true vegetarian. After dinner, I went to gaze at the stars, study Kiswahili, and then sleep.

TUESDAY, JULY 29, 1997 (AUNT IRENE'S BIRTHDAY)

Last night, I was asleep shortly after nine o'clock, but there was an unusual interruption. The guests that David had looked for earlier in Itaka had come, so they were talking for a while. I imagine it was around 11:00 p.m. I finally went back to sleep and was awakened at 4:20 a.m. Surprisingly, I went back to sleep, but I heard David leave at 6:00 a.m. Finally, at 6:40 I got up, dressed, and woke the guys. We had our usual chai and mandazi. Then it was off to the village on foot. We started at 7:45, and what a safari it was. Aknaktum had his music and led the way most of the time, about seventy-five feet ahead. Ron and I were together until the third turn. Then, I was lagging about fifty feet from Ron, and he was about forty feet from Aknaktum. It was an exhausting walk for me. Toward the end, Ron led us in, followed by

Aknaktum and me, the final leg. Whew! I was really tired, as if it was a day's work already to walk about four miles within one and a half hours. It seemed so much more difficult to walk to the village than it did to walk back to the farm. I really didn't want to walk to the village again, but if I had to, I would. When we arrived at the work site at quarter to ten, we assembled the materials and tools and mixed a large amount of cement. I joined in, even though I was already tired. However, once I started work, it wasn't that bad. I did some of everything—carried cement, hauled bricks to the fundi, and kept the cement watered. Today we built on the long backside and raised it by four bricks. There were 160 bricks laid, and I must have handled close to one-third of them. We finished at 12:40 p.m. and went to Howard's for lunch. I was truly physically spent. Howard's wife, Marcia, had made some home brew (beer), so I decided to try it. It smelled like beer, looked like chocolate milk, and tasted like, well, I still don't know. I did get a slight buzz for a few minutes from it, but then its effect was lost.

Lunch was served—rice and the tiny dried fish, cooked with a tinge of cabbage in a sauce. We each had an individual bowl of rice. I was the last to finish, I guess because of the small pitcher of home brew. Afterward, Ron and I fell asleep while Aknaktum was outside reading his *Source* magazine. I was happily surprised when I was awakened from my short slumber because Shomptie had arrived to drive us back to the farm. It was quarter to three, and we were not expecting him until four o'clock. When we arrived at three thirty, I went straight to my area, changed from my work clothes into some shorts and T-shirt, and fell asleep as I touched my bed. I got up from the nap at five o'clock and started to catch up with my journal. I wrote that I hoped Aunt Irene was having a nice birthday. I was sure that she knew my heart and love were with her.)

We had the usual dinner, chai and mandazi. When David arrived at about 7:15, we were quite elated because we were certain that he had mailed our letters and brought us bottled water. However, we were all disappointed when David said that he forgot to go to the post office and also forgot to purchase the water. Ronnie was particularly unhappy. Nevertheless, David did promise to boil us some water for the next day. The nocturnal activities were as usual, thinking about all sorts of things, dreaming, going for the urination, and waking early in the morning.

WEDNESDAY, JULY 30, 1997

I got out of bed a little later than usual, around 7:20. David said that he would drive us to the village, leaving at eight o'clock, but he was going on to Mbeya and would not return until tomorrow evening. Therefore, we would have to walk back. The jeep's starter was defective, so we would have to push it for a jump-start. After going down the hill without starting, and David summoning three workers to help push it up the hill, the jeep finally started, and it went down the hill into the coffee tree grove. When we reached the village at Howard's *duka* (his shop), we were informed that there would be no work because the chief fundi's relative had died, and there would be the funeral and mourning. We were happy in one sense but disappointed in another. Since we were there at the site, we decided to do something, so we worked on the foundation. We started to fill in rocks on the leveled side. We threw rocks and broken bricks until this side was saturated. Then we worked on the other side for a short while. David returned and said that he wasn't going to Mbeya until later, so he could take us back. We stopped by Howard's for a few minutes and then returned to the farm in the early afternoon. We waited a long time for our lunch since David's relatives, brother-in-law, and father-in-law had to be fed. David's father-in-law had been traveling with him during the morning. Lunch was rice, beans, and cabbage, and we ate practically all of it, Aknaktum having only cabbage and rice. Later in the afternoon we leisurely rested, read, and discussed issues such as slavery and Africa's development. We started having our baths around six o'clock, shortly before sunset.

Later, I listened to the radio in Kiswahili but didn't understand anything. As mentioned, the radio was powered by electricity from David's solar energy system. Solar energy development and implementation were the appropriate directions, especially for rural Africa. I would like to examine long-term ramifications of this potential venture. As I was writing in my journal, a rat ran out in front of me but went back. They usually didn't come out until eight o'clock or later, roaming about precisely when we are having dinner. I had the usual dinner and the usual night.

THURSDAY, JULY 31,1997

The morning started at 7:20 with the usual routine. Since David had left with the jeep, we had to walk to the village, another ninety-minute journey. We started at eight o'clock and arrived around nine thirty or so. Those hills were treacherous, and my body paid the price. I was so tired that I didn't want to think about working. To make things worse, it appeared that there would be only the fundis and us. We alone would have to do a lot of the cement mixing, carrying it and bricks, and all the other labor. We had to chisel out some bricks that had been laid on the back wall because the fundis had forgotten to leave spaces for the windows. After this was done, we set the windows and started to cement around them. I was really tired after the walk and a breakfast of only tea and bread. I tried to do my part, but I was taking more breaks than usual. We had to wait for the water, cement, and tools, but I wasn't complaining. I was not eager to work in the hot sun after walking four miles up and down a mountainous terrain. However, we did get the windows in place and some additional bricks laid. It was a good day's work after all. We had lunch at Howard's around three o'clock—rice and beans again. Then we started walking back around five o'clock, arriving shortly after six thirty. It was just past seven thirty when I got ready to have tea and then bathe. Ron and Aknaktum had bathed already. After the bath, it was the usual dinner and then to bed. However, Ronnie and I stayed up until around ten thirty, talking about the college, people— women, in particular—and all sorts of other things.

FRIDAY, AUGUST 1, 1997

This was the second consecutive day that we had to walk the four miles to the village and back. Aknaktum said that his knees had given out on him so he did not go. Ronnie and I made the trek, but he seemed less spirited than the earlier trips. In fact, he was walking at my pace and barely keeping up. We arrived at 10:00 a.m. and were happy to see that the work had already begun. There were several young men assisting the fundis, and since Ron and I were tired from the walk, we were not eager to get involved. We did our share, though, as the windows were placed in the front, and bricks were laid around them. The door frame was adjusted to fit. We ended work around two thirty and went to Howard's to have lunch. I had already requested ugali, so we had that dish with the tiny fish in a sauce. We rested up until around five o'clock and then started the safari back to the farm. We tried several different routes that we thought were shortcuts, and we got slightly lost several different times. Finally, we arrived at the farm around seven thirty, an hour later than usual, totally exhausted. It was a bath, chai and mandazi for dinner, and then the bed.

SATURDAY, AUGUST 2, 1997

The day started routinely. We walked reluctantly to the village to do a half day's work, but no one had come to the site. It was shortly after nine thirty, and imagine the disappointment, not so much of not working but that we had walked to the village unnecessarily and now had to walk back. The guys were ready to head directly back. I wanted to wait until later, so I decided to have a beer—yes, early in the morning—and then make the trek with the guys. The sun was getting hotter but not too hot. We arrived back at around 11:45. Just think about walking four miles one way and four miles back in less than four hours. In the afternoon, we simply relaxed, read, had lunch, and had dinner later. There was some excitement for a while.

As I lay resting, I heard a crackling noise. At first I thought it was rain; then I went outside and saw there was a brush fire all around the back and on one side of the house. It was really flaming and generating heat. The housekeeper, Upenda, and the girls were not too excited about it; I didn't get too alarmed but remained cautious. It burned for about ten minutes, then subsided, and eventually extinguished itself for the most part. The girls played in the residue.

Later in the evening, around eight thirty, David arrived with our water and said he had mailed our letters. We talked with him, had dinner, and went to bed. I was surprised that it seemed that I had an unusual night. I didn't wake up in the middle of the night to urinate, nor did I stay awake a few hours thinking. I didn't even remember having strange dreams, such as negotiating with my estranged wife for a divorce. I got up for the first time after seven thirty the next morning and returned to bed for additional rest.

SUNDAY, AUGUST 3, 1997

After a much-needed late sleep, I got out of bed around 8:40 a.m. We settled the account with David for purchasing the water and for mailing the letters. We had our breakfast and discussed selling coffee in the States as a joint venture with David. At eleven o'clock I went to the river to wash clothes. It was fun going in the jeep to the river. I had quite a few things to wash—my work clothes, towel, bath cloth, sweat suit, six pairs of underwear, three pairs of tube socks, hats. I wore shorts and sandals so that I could get into the water and seriously wash. David took us to a good spot, and we got to it: soaked the clothes, beat them on the rocks, washed them with detergent (Tide that I had brought), and then rinsed them. I even discovered that I could use a small rock to scrub out the dirt. This was relaxing and fun. I think that I got at least 95 percent of the dirt out. There were a few things that I didn't clean as well as I wanted because I was the last to finish. We returned and hung up the clothes.

Later, we had lunch: rice, carrots, string beans, and red beans. In the afternoon, we read and rested. I took a bath and I even shaved my moustache, but I didn't have a mirror to see how I looked. Then I enjoyed my last beer (I had two for the weekend) and listened to Luther Vandross on tape.

MONDAY, AUGUST 4, 1997

Shomptie drove us to the village, and—surprisingly—I missed walking up the challenging hill. However, as the jeep was plodding up the hill, I was panting as I rode in the car. At the site, we did our usual—mixing cement, carrying bricks, bringing water. Lunch at Howard's was ugali and cabbage. The lunch was excellent; the cabbage was chopped and cooked in peanut oil. Ron and I ate so much that we had to take a rest before the walk back. Aknaktum left once he heard "ugali for lunch," and he was lucky enough to hitch a ride back with Shomptie. When Ron and I got back, we learned we couldn't take a bath because there was no water, so Shomptie took the jeep with buckets and the drum to fetch water. He returned very late so we didn't bathe that night.

The night began as usual—we went to bed around quarter after nine—but in the middle of the night, the rats were having a fight in the ceiling, directly above my head. We all woke up in unison and wanted to know what the hell was going on. It was funny but disturbing. Since I woke up so startled, I found it difficult to relax and go back to sleep. I struggled but didn't get some winks until about four thirty.

TUESDAY, AUGUST 5, 1997

After the rough night, we started the morning with a nice hot bath. It was refreshing since the previous night I'd had less than a complete and peaceful sleep. After breakfast, we walked to the village, and I had the confrontation with my nemesis, the steep mountain. We made it but were tired. After taking a short rest at Howard's, we headed for the work site. There was only one fundi on site, so we had to help him mix cement and prepare for the day's work. Obviously, we were not eager to do the work by ourselves after the hour and a half walk. Nevertheless, our commitment prevailed, and we assisted in completing one corner until another fundi came. We worked more rapidly and completed the other corners as well as on that particular side of the structure. In spite of it all, we were satisfied with the work of the day. We then went to Howard's for lunch.

As we waited, one of the fundis invited me to accompany him to the house next door and have some home brew. I accepted his invitation and enjoyed several gulps from the large communal cup. The people there were surprised that I drank with them but didn't get drunk. They spoke in Kiswahili, and I didn't understand anything. I later went back for lunch—ugali and small dried fish stew. It was delicious. After resting and talking about rap music, the guys and I hit the trail back to the farm. The walk back always seemed more manageable because we came down that mountain. We arrived, had our baths, and ate dinner. At bedtime, I prepared for the rats. One had come out earlier and approached me as I wrote in my journal. I was glad that I frightened it back.

Friday of this week would be a holiday, so there would be no work for us. Moreover, Saturday also would be a day off, so I'd be able to maintain my strength for those two days. Before rodent time, a short part of the evening was involved in a potential sale of some of my clothes that I didn't want to bring back: a pair of green slacks, a green striped shirt, and a V-neck T-shirt. I planned to complete the sale to Alosie, David's brother-in-law, the next day.

WEDNESDAY, AUGUST 6, 1997

We were fortunate enough to get a ride with Shomptie, but we had to travel around, as he had to pick up coffee from certain individuals so that it could be weighed. We finally arrived at the work site and were surprised to see so many people there. Many young men were mixing cement, four fundis were laying bricks, women were bringing water, and others were sitting around with a large pail of home brew. People were working diligently, so we joined the labor party and worked hard ourselves, and then we were invited to have some home brew along with the others. Ron and I accepted.

We worked assiduously until about 3:35. This was the longest and most productive day we'd had—we completed the front and back walls. As a result, the height of the structure also was complete.

We later met Shomptie and rode back with him. Aknaktum decided to cook the spaghetti that David had brought earlier. I opened some of my tuna to share. As I mentioned, the guys didn't eat tuna, but the housekeeper, Upenda, and the girls ate some of it. It was an interesting dinner for me: spaghetti with tomato sauce, tuna, and red beans, all mixed together.

Earlier, Ron and I had taken some clothing for Howard to sell at the store. We indicated a price for each item. This was a little exciting, just to see if there would be any offers.

The night was unusually warm, and I was up several times, urinating, more than ordinary. I guess it was the home brew.

THURSDAY, AUGUST 7, 1997

It was a day to walk in and back again. I mustered up energy, hoping that this would be the last time for walking. Remember, Friday was to be a holiday, which meant no work, and Saturdays were always questionable, even though we were assured that there would be work this Saturday. We took the usual walk, but I had to stop to defecate. As I squatted, the grass was sticking up around my buttocks and everywhere else. After this crude elimination, I handled the hill rather well. When we arrived at the site, work was underway with a few people—only two fundis and four or five others. The children had brought bricks inside so that the walls and doors could be done for the separate rooms. We were reluctant to begin, as the walk had taken its toll on our bodies. Nevertheless, I went to assist, mixing cement and carrying it to the fundis. After about forty-five minutes, I felt very faint and weak. I decided to go to Howard's early. I thought I might have sunstroke. I rested there and had lunch. Then Ron and Aknaktum came and had lunch. As we rested, people came by to see the clothes we had for sale. I sold two shirts, and Ron sold a pair of pants. At four thirty, we started the return walk. I stopped by the river to soak my feet and refresh myself. Afterward, I felt great and walked back spiritedly.

FRIDAY, AUGUST 8, 1997

Because it was a holiday, we planned to go to the village for the festival and celebration. Shomptie picked us up around two thirty, and we went with the girls, Alosie, and another fellow from the farm. As we arrived in the village, we noticed that everyone was dressed in their best clothing. We stopped at Howard's for a while; then we went down to the celebration. There were lots of people, including many children. Adults were drinking beer (both home brew and bottled) and conversing inside and outside the bar. The children were playing and watching. I had some beer and joined the party. It was amazing to see men dancing with each other, grinding and winding on top of each other, but no one was gay. I thought that people here would not understand the concept of homosexuality, so obviously dancing this way was not a problem for them. A man asked me to dance, and I accepted. This reminded me of my experience in Ghana, some twenty-five years ago. We danced, and I was glad that we remained apart because I am not accustomed to dancing with men. He invited me to dance with women at the same time. It was an enjoyable evening. We returned to the farm, had a late dinner, and then retired for the evening.

SATURDAY, AUGUST 9, 1997

Shomptie came to pick us up around nine thirty in the morning, and we headed to the village, expecting to do our last day of work. At the work site, however, only the roof fundi was present. I was surprised to see that the frame for the roof had been put in place, evidently on the holiday. However, some strips had to be put in place, so we helped the fundi and his assistant in this task. Once this was done, the next job was to put on the tin roof, but we couldn't find the galvanized nails for the chore. I was quite disappointed because I would have liked to have seen the somewhat finished product. I hoped we could complete it on Monday before we left for the States.

We left the site and had lunch at Howard's. I was happy to learn that Pearson, one of the fundis, had bought my boots for $12,000 shingili. He had paid $10,000, and the other $2,000 was forthcoming. After lunch, we rested for a short while and then started our walk back to the farm. I was wearing my sandals, so I got dirt all over my feet and sandals, just like the people of the village, yet it was a wonderful sensation to walk without the heavy work boots. When we reached the last little store that had beer (Howard and the other stores didn't have any.), I stopped to have one; guys went on ahead of me. I wanted to be alone, and I particularly did not want to hear all of Aknaktum's complaints and dissatisfaction.

I was looking forward to making the last half of the journey alone. Shortly after resuming the hike, I met Shomptie, who was walking and carrying the little shy girl who was afraid of us. He invited me to go back and have some home brew, but I declined. I continued the walk, and when I reached the last river, I decided to wash my feet and relax. It was enjoyable listening to the water and scraping dead skin from my feet. As I was leaving, Brison, one of the fundis, came to draw water. As we talked—he in Kiswahili and a little English, and I in English and practically no Kiswahili—he invited me to his house, which wasn't too far from David's farm. Brison rode his bike with the water on his back.

He went up the hill as if he were flying, but I was panting as I tried to keep up with him on foot.

His farm had coffee, cattle, and chickens and was very nice. He had five children, ages four to fourteen. We sat for about an hour, having beer and peanuts. I took some pictures of him and his children; then he walked me to the path back toward David's farm.

I came in and met the guys getting ready to take their baths. I started writing in my journal. For dinner, we had tea and something other than mandazi—chapati, an unleavened bread.

SUNDAY, AUGUST 10, 1997

Saturday night was very difficult for me because I was up literally every hour or ninety minutes, urinating. I don't know if it was because I had the first beer early in the day and then some home brew at Brison's, another beer, and tea and probably a little water. I had taken a diuretic earlier that morning; nevertheless, the urine had to be expelled on schedule. I was up at least seven times from ten at night to seven thirty in the morning. When I finally got up for good, I was surprised to see David and was happy to hear his voice. I asked him about the Roots group (these were the individuals who had organized the project in which we were engaged). Young children were traveling with them also. He explained that they were on their way from Mbeya and would be at the village for the day. We would meet them there and make our final departure with them. I was overjoyed but deeply saddened at the same time. I was ambivalent about packing because I would be preparing to leave the place that had been home for me for almost three weeks. I thought that we would meet the Roots group in the village and leave from there, so we packed completely and placed our luggage in the jeep for the final trip. Then David explained that the Roots group was coming to the farm, and we would all leave after that.

We left for the village just after nine thirty, and when we reached the middle of the village, we encountered the bus with the Roots group.

We changed from the jeep to the bus and went back to the site of the school and library. The villagers were staring at the people who got on and off the bus. Several of the village officials came to greet the group. We went over to the school, where one room was being used for a religious service. Then we went to the library site, and we explained all the work we had done. There were many opportunities to take photographs. I took pictures, acting like a tourist rather than the construction worker I had been for the past few weeks. Later, we took the bus to the farm, and David, standing in front of the warehouse, explained the coffee growing and processing business. Then we went to the housing complex, including the Roots house, which I had not seen before. We returned, had refreshments, and discussed many issues as we waited for lunch.

We had a nice lunch, prepared by Upenda; Howard's wife, who had come along; and David's wife, who was on the Roots bus with their two younger children—their daughter, Fermi, and their son, Jackie, who was about eighteen months old. After lunch we started back to the village and to Mbeya. Leaving was a certainty at that point. Happiness and sadness still overshadowed me. When we reached the village, the three of us, Aknaktum, Ron and I, stopped at Howard's to finalize our business with the clothing and other items. I ended up leaving most of the things to be sold, and I told Howard to keep the proceeds and share them with the village. Then it was on to the bus to Mbeya. As it had been so long since we had come to Mbeya that I'd forgotten how dusty the road was. Still, I could hardly believe that we were actually leaving. We made the journey in about two and a half hours, arriving in Mbeya around eight thirty that night. We checked into the hotel where the Roots group was, had dinner, and took a shower with hot water. What a joy!

Earlier, Ron and I had made arrangements for David and Michael, the leader of the Roots group, to purchase tickets for us on the train that was to take us to Dar Es Salam. Aknaktum had planned to go by bus. However, he changed his mind and now wanted to go on the train.

As I wrote in my journal, I heard music from a disco below my hotel room. It was very loud, and I wondered how I would sleep. The hotel seemed a strange place for me, not being on a mattress on the floor, not having Ron and Aknaktum sleeping in the same room, and not hearing rats. I finally got tired and tried to sleep at 12:35 a.m.

MONDAY, AUGUST 11, 1997

I got a reasonably good night's sleep in a fairly decent hotel in Mbeya. I got up shortly before eight o'clock and repacked and organized my things. Ron came to my room, and we decided to find a local restaurant for breakfast. We walked up the hill and encountered some of the people from the Roots group. They were leaving around ten o'clock to travel by bus to Malawi. We all went to the bank to exchange money. Then Ron and I found a local restaurant, where we ate hot cereal and chapati. When we arrived back at the hotel, we expected to see David and Michael with our train tickets to Dar, but we were surprised to find that train was scheduled for the following day. So, we were to spend another day in Mbeya.

The students and I decided to purchase the tickets ourselves to ensure that we'd have seats. Ron went back to the hotel, and Aknaktum and I went for a walk. We walked by the market, and I bought a piece of cloth. We wanted to go to the bus station, where we could check on the price of the rooming house rather than paying the hotel price for another night. As I was asking a police officer for directions to the bus station, Aknaktum snapped a picture of us. The officer became furious, saying to Aknaktum, "Who gave you permission to take a picture of me? Give me your camera. You owe me 50,000 1=." Tanzanian currency is shingilis. 50,000 1= Shingilis were equivalent to about $40.00 dollars at that time. We did not know what was happening, but the officer slowly explained that it was an offense to take pictures, particularly of police officers, without getting permission. He took Aknaktum to the mini-police station and demanded he pay the fine. Aknaktum didn't have the money with him, so I had to go to the hotel and get his travelers checks. Then he went to the bank, exchanged money, and paid the officer. I suspected that things were not on the up and up, but I didn't say anything. I didn't want more trouble, and it was time for Aknaktum to learn a lesson. After taking the film, the officer returned the camera, and we left.

We went to the bus station area, where we both had beverages, and I also had some chips and eggs. Then we visited Omar Shariff, our initial liaison in Mbeya. Later, we examined the guest house and decided to rent a room where the three of us could stay and pay 2,000 1= shingilis instead of 35,000 1= at the hotel. This was a dramatic drop in the price, from about$27.00 to less than $5.00. We returned and told Ron the news, and he was satisfied. We prepared to make the move around five o'clock.

When we arrived at the bus station, Ron and I decided to have some fish and chips with eggs. We received the fish and chips but there were no eggs mixed with the chips. I was content to have just fish and chips, but Ron had to have his chips with eggs. We waited and waited, and he finally got them. Then we went to the room we were sharing. There were only two beds; the manager could not put another bed in the room. Ron always had his sleeping bag, so with Aknaktum's comforter, he slept on a raised area under a high window. We slept fairly well through the night, but I had to visit the bathroom, which was clean but smelly, several times during the night. It was fortunate that our room was not too far from the bathroom, but unfortunate because of the odor from it.

TUESDAY, AUGUST 12, 1997

(Happy twenty-ninth birthday, Tomia, my sweet and lovely daughter.)

When we left our "Port Authority" sleeping area, we proceeded to the African Cultural Shop that we had seen as we were walking to the guest house. Ron purchased a walking cane, and we remained there and conversed with the proprietor, who had many artifacts, mainly from Malawi. I bought a staff with a female figure carved on it and a Maasai bracelet. The final negotiation was the trading of a water bottle for a cowry shell bracelet. We returned to the rooming house, attended to bodily needs, procured our luggage, and took a taxi to the train station.

The train was scheduled to leave at quarter after one that afternoon, but we didn't depart until around two thirty. The twenty-four-hour train ride was interesting. We took second class, a cabin of six persons, so we shared the space with a Danish couple and a young, quiet Caucasian guy. The cabin was unbelievably hot, so I spent a lot of time in the dining car. I would sit and stare out of the windows. The food was adequate, so I ate my usual meal. At night, we all slept on the bed boards, six of them. We arrived in Dar Es Salam safely the next afternoon. We immediately headed for the airport to make certain that we had adequate time to go through customs and be ready for our evening flight back to the States.

When it was departure time, we were informed that our KLM flight was overbooked, and the airline was offering two hundred dollars for passengers who were willing to forego this flight and leave the following afternoon. In addition, the airline would provide hotel accommodations for the night and an unlimited meal voucher. Ron and I reasoned that being away one more day when we'd been away over a month already was not a big deal, and receiving the amenities was worth it. Aknaktum decided not to give up his seat. Since his parents were paying his expenses, these perks had no significance for him. What a spoiled grown brat!

Ron and I enjoyed our last night in Tanzania in style. The hotel was a luxurious one, with a comfortable bed with sheets and pillows, a hot shower, and air conditioning. When we entered the five-star restaurant, it was a beautiful sight. We were served by elegant and professional waiters. I ordered prawns, and it was the first time in my life that I'd had such juicy and delicious shrimp. Ron had a filet mignon dinner.

We even ordered wine, which we thought we would have to pay for separately, but it was all included. After having such a scrumptious meal and sleeping in a chamber designed for royalty, we considered the flight back to JFK as heavenly.

The final activity of this project was the submitting of papers for the students' field experiences along with their analyses and, subsequently, the assignment of grades.

CHAPTER 10

POST-PROFESSORIATE TRAVEL TO GHANA

A fter returning from the summer travel of 1997, I resumed my duties as professor, served as chairperson of the Psychology Department, and subsequently was appointed as interim dean of the School of Liberal Arts and Education. At the end -of the spring semester of 2006, I retired from Medgar Evers College after a thirty-five-year tenure.

I resumed my friendship with a Ghanaian, Don Otchere, who had come to the States in the 1970s, lived in my house, and later moved to the Midwest. He presently owns a ranch in San Antonio, Texas, has an environmental compliance business, and travels to Ghana at least annually. He invited me to accompany him to Ghana in April 2010. As I was desirous to visit the homeland after so many years of absence, I accepted the invitation.

RETURN TO GHANA—2010

WEDNESDAY, APRIL 21, 2010

I arrived at JFK International Airport at 12:50 p.m., and by 1:15 I had checked in and was at the gate. I had plenty of time to wait for my flight, scheduled for 4:45. As I sat waiting, I decided to write a letter to a church member, instructing her on some issues that had to be taken care of while I was away. Incidentally, I was serving as president of one of the steward divisions of my church, the Greater Allen African Methodist Episcopal Cathedral of New York. Once the letter was composed, I concluded that I must mail it before departure. There were no places to purchase stamps or to post the letter at Terminal 3, but I learned that I could purchase stamps and mail the letter at Terminal 4. I had almost two hours before check-in, so I went to Terminal 4, completed the task, and returned to Terminal 3. That meant, however, that I had to return through security. There was a rather long line, but I eventually passed through with plenty of time before the flight. I sat and waited until boarding time. I also was waiting for Don, who was arriving on a connecting flight from San Antonio. He appeared as boarding started. We exchanged greetings and joined the queue to board the plane. His seat was in row 21, and mine was in row 25.

The flight was relatively smooth once we departed, but we were delayed because the luggage of a traveler who was not taking the flight had to be removed. In the air, we were served dinner with a choice of beverage, including wine or beer. I opted for wine. Early in the morning we were served breakfast. Because I had requested a special meal for dinner (seafood), I also received a special breakfast, before the other passengers were served.

THURSDAY, APRIL 22, 2010

Once we arrived at Accra and went through customs, we were met by Don's friend and other relatives who were waiting at the airport. We loaded our luggage into a taxi and were driven to the house of another of Don's friends, who had a car for us to use during our time in Ghana. Once we left Accra, we were on our way to Nsawan. When we arrived there, the car was taken to a mechanic, not at a service station but in a residential area where cars were repaired. The mechanic was skillful and in a short while the air conditioning was fixed. We then visited Don's sister-in-law, who prepared an enjoyable dinner for us. Afterward, we eventually arrived at the house where we would be staying. I was indeed happy to see a bed where I could stretch out and sleep. It was a wonderful night of sleep in Ghana.

FRIDAY, APRIL 23, 2010

I awoke early and went for a walk with Don, aka Osae, who visited some relatives he hadn't seen for a long time. He also showed me the house where he was born. Then we returned and had breakfast. Later, we traveled to Aburi and other local villages. There, he informed his relatives that he would be enstooled as chief. In each village, the elders were gathered to discuss the proceedings. Libation with a bottle of alcohol was conducted, including each person taking a sip from the same glass. Then each person was given his or her own portion from the bottle. We visited a few villages, going up and down terrible roads that were desperately in need of repair. We returned, had dinner, and went to bed.

SATURDAY, APRIL 24, 2010

We went to Accra in the morning to exchange money. I was asked if I wanted to participate in the enstoolment ceremony, and I agreed. (I didn't know exactly what I was getting into.) Initially, I had to purchase a piece of cloth, special sandals, wrist bands, and an ornamental necklace. These cost about one hundred dollars. Next, I was asked to contribute four hundred dollars as my portion for the ceremony. I was shocked but gave up the money. I asked if there was anything else that required more money, but that was it. We left Accra and went back to Aburi to make additional preparations for the ceremony, which was to be held on Monday. We also visited other villages on our way back.

SUNDAY, APRIL 25, 2010

We relaxed for the morning and later visited Osae's sister-in-law, Mary. Afterward, we visited another village and went through the same protocol of pouring libation. I was taken to sacred shrines where Osae and I were presented to the ancestry. It was such a humbling experience. We returned and waited for his friend from Nebraska, Greg Nelson, to arrive. He was picked up at the airport by the same friend who had met us. Greg came to the house and settled in.

MONDAY, APRIL 26, 2010

THE BIG CEREMONY

We awoke early, had breakfast, and waited to be picked up. Greg agreed to be part of the ceremony, even though he was much more in the dark than I was because he had just arrived the previous evening. Borrowed ceremonial clothing and accessories were provided for him. When the transportation arrived for us, we were taken to a house; we sat in the living room while others arrived for the event. We were told to wear only shorts and a shirt and not to bring valuables with us. When things got started, we were told to take off all clothing except our shorts. We were given old dashikis (a type of loose-fitting, pullover shirt) to wear; then we continued to wait. All of a sudden, a woman came in and dusted us with baby powder all over our faces, legs, arms, and everywhere. We were then led outside. As we reached the porch, we were each told to bend down and mount the shoulders, individually, of a young man. At the same time, a patch of grass was placed in our mouths. We were paraded through the streets with one young man carrying each of us and two others on each side holding our out-stretched arms. The young fellow carrying me appeared to weigh about 135 pounds, and I weighed over two hundred pounds. All I could think was, *Please don't let me fall.* Midway to the community center, another young man took over the task, but he was no bigger. We arrived at the town meeting center, dismounted from the shoulders of our carriers, and were led to the council hall. We sat on the floor, still with the grass in our mouths and the powder all over us. There was libation and a meeting of the elders, speaking in Twi, a language I didn't understand.

Next, we were led to a car that would transport us to the major town, Aburi. When we arrived at the meeting area of the village, there was a festive atmosphere. Chairs were placed all around, and most of the villagers were attired in their best ceremonial clothing. We were placed on public display, still with the grass in our mouths. The elders and others gathered around; libations were poured to the ancestors at the public shrine. We were then seated near the shrine, where a young sheep was killed and its blood was spilled over our feet and legs. I can still remember the sensation of the warm blood of the lamb splattering on me.

There were more libations and dedications. Later, we were led to a bathroom inside the compound, where we were allowed to bathe, washing off the lamb's blood, the dirt, and everything else with cold water. Once we cleaned up, we were dressed in our ceremonial clothing, Ashanti cloth, sandals, and accessories. As we were presented to the public, we received thunderous applause. There were more libations and dedications as we sat in our ceremonial chairs. We were officially presented to the chief of the village and other elders, as the master of ceremonies gave a brief statement about each of us. We were assigned our new names—for me, Yaw Adu Paarko I, and I was enstooled as *fotosanhene*, meaning finance minister of the village. As part of the ceremony, we had to sit three times on the lap of the chief. Then we had to do an individual dance to the drum music that was played. This concluded the major part of the ceremony, and we then were official *nanas* (chiefs). Everyone congratulated us. Later, we had drinks and food, which was supplied by the money we had contributed. We finally left Aburi after an exhausting day.

Dr. Thomas O. Edwards enstooled as Nana Adu Paarko I.

WEDNESDAY, APRIL 28, 2010

After breakfast we took a trip to Accra to exchange money. We also went to the tourist market where I saw lots of interesting souvenirs and other potential gifts. We relaxed and had some refreshments before leaving for Aburi. There, we met the local chief, who confirmed our enstoolment titles and names. We had some drinks and then returned home.

THURSDAY, APRIL 29, 2010

Greg and I walked to the post office, found the Commercial Bank with an ATM, and withdrew money. On the return, we stopped by Patience's shop, took photos, and had some ground nuts (peanuts). Patience was a young lady friend of Osae's family, who operated a beauty supply store.

SUNDAY, MAY 2, 2010

Greg and I went to church with Patience and Ama, Osae's niece, who cooked for us while we were there. It was a small local Methodist church, where there was inspirational singing by various youth groups. The sermon was in Twi, but there were occasional English translations. We were introduced, asked to come forward, and encouraged to say a few words. Everyone thought that I was Ghanaian. We left early so that we could return to Aburi and prepare for our official enstoolment, a presentation to the head chief, the *aburihene*, of the entire region of Aburi. We finally left at two thirty for a three o'clock ceremony. It took more than forty-five minutes for the journey, and we had to check-in at the guest house of the Aburi Botanical Gardens and get dressed in our formal ceremonial attire. Once we arrived at the local chief's place, we went through other formalities, including presenting the chief with gifts (money and a bottle of schnapps).

We then went to the aburihene's residence, where we waited for almost an hour in light rain before he came. Our presentations were only a small part of the total meeting. After the formal protocol and after our names were confirmed, we went to greet the chief. We sat on his lap three times, did a little dance, and received our charges. Once our activities were completed, there were other matters to be attended at the gathering, including informing the chief of two deaths and the respective funeral arrangements. Then, there was a protracted discussion about the conditions of the roads, particularly the one between Nsawam and Aburi. The lack of progress was attributed to politics, one party's accusing the other for the delay; the contractors who were Chinese; and a host of other excuses.

When these proceedings were concluded, we returned to the guest house, changed clothing, and went out to find food. It was after nine o'clock, and all we could find were the local indigenous shops. Osae and I had fried yams and fish; Greg had an omelet. It wasn't the best, but it was food. We retired in our rooms at the guest house, which had no running water. There were lights in some rooms but not in others. I could deduce that once upon a time the guest house was a nice place, but when we visited it showed serious neglect. I did sleep well.

MONDAY, MAY 3, 2010

We toured the facility of the Aburi Botanical Gardens and observed the plants and trees on the premises. We later had breakfast, which was delicious. At least the restaurant was maintained in suitable condition. I had fried rice and fish and drank beer—yes, for breakfast. We returned to Nsawam and relaxed for a good portion of the afternoon. I accompanied Greg to the bank, but he was unable to perform his transaction.

TUESDAY, MAY 4, 2010

I took my three-mile walk in the morning. Greg and I went to the bank, and he was able to get money. We also exchanged dollars at another location. We went to the local health clinic and met a Caucasian nurse from San Antonio, Texas, who was the administrator. She had been in Ghana for more than twenty-three years. This was the clinic where Osae's sister-in-law, the midwife, worked. As we discussed various issues, we drank coconut water. After leaving the premises, we went to the post office to buy stamps; then we bought envelopes at a local store and returned home. I drank some local alcoholic drink and became wobbly. I took a long nap, awoke for dinner, and then had a more familiar drink, a little Chivas Regal.

WEDNESDAY, MAY 5, 2010

I took a long walk alone before breakfast and became very nauseated before I finished eating. I regurgitated my entire breakfast, had diarrhea, and felt terrible for most of the morning. Greg gave me some medication for diarrhea, and it made me feel better. Osae's niece Ama also made a special soup for me. I did feel better after resting for a while. Osae had gone to Accra to purchase plumbing supplies and when he returned, he invited me to have palm wine with his guests who had arrived earlier. We had already invited them to have beer. After having the palm wine, we were invited to Kwesi's house for dinner. Kwesi was Osae's nephew, and he had assisted in many of our activities. We started walking to Kwesi's. I thought it would be a short distance, but it took about forty-five minutes through back roads and paths. For dinner, we had a corn mixture—the texture resembled grits—and chicken stew that contained okra and some delicious spices. We ate African style, with our hands from a communal bowl. It was a nice gesture on Kwesi's part.

THURSDAY, MAY 6, 2010

It was great to have yams and fish sauce for breakfast. I took it easy this morning, reading *Smart Money* magazine, which I had brought with me, writing letters, and trying to remain cool. The day was rather peacefully as we prepared for Greg's departure. He left a few items for me, including the diarrhea medication. We also traded money: he had two hundred Ghanaian cedis, which traded for about 140 US dollars. Hannah, Patience, and Ama prepared a special departure dinner. It was an excellent meal. The taxi came for Greg, and we said good-bye. The women were disappointed because he didn't leave any tips (money) for them, but he did leave some Nebraska T-shirts, pens, and other items. Nana Afua called Greg as he was on his way to the airport because he departed with the articles he had used in the ceremony but did not purchase. The taxi driver was told to return the items that Greg had. The rest of the evening was spent with the women, discussing Greg's lack of considerateness.

FRIDAY, MAY 7, 2010

Osae and I headed to Kumasi very early in the morning. We were accompanied by two young women: the daughter of the woman who rented a portion of Osae's house and her friend. For the four-and-a-half-hour trip, the travel was rough in the beginning because of the poor road conditions, but as we journeyed the roads improved. I was hungry, but we didn't stop until we reached our destination. We arrived at Nana Afua's brother's, Kwaduo Appiah's, house, which was a nice two-story building with all the rooms on the second floor. The family had all the modern conveniences: television, a beautifully decorated living room, a balcony, a bathroom with shower, and two toilets. We enjoyed a delicious lunch there; then we went to visit some of Osae's relatives. The evening was relatively quiet, and I watched television for the first time since arriving in Ghana; it was primarily soccer. While at this residence, I tried to take photographs, but my camera battery was dying.

SATURDAY, MAY 8, 2010

In the morning, the young ladies assisted in preparing breakfast but were concerned about not having an extra change of clothing; they'd thought there would be only one overnight stay, and so did I. There was a boutique downstairs, so Osae purchased each of them a new outfit—a dressy top with matching jeans. After this was done, one of the girls realized that she had to work the following day, so they had to leave anyway. We drove them to the bus station, and they departed. We then went to the post office, where I purchased stamps. We found vendors with postcards across the street. Later, we visited Kwaduo Appiah's office, which was air conditioned and very comfortable. He had a computer and was the manager of a fruit juice shipping company. We left his office and went to a chop bar (restaurant) for lunch. I had fufu with fish and sauce. Fufu has to be eaten with the hands and dipped in sauce before swallowing. I enjoyed it and chased it with a beer. We returned to his office and waited for him to end work at two o'clock. We also waited for a relative of Osae's, who arrived around four o'clock. We then went to visit her family, who were Seventh-day Adventists. Surprisingly, there were many Muslims in the same community. We remained there until dark and then left for the house. Being tired after a busy day, I showered and went to bed.

SUNDAY, MAY 9, 2010

We were up early, had breakfast, and talked about various subjects, including the Bible and religion. Osae's relatives, the Seventh-day Adventists, arrived. Osae and Kwadwo went for a walk as I ironed my clothes, which I'd washed the previous day since I brought only one change of clothing. When they returned, we had more discussions.

Initially, the family planned to go to church, but this did not happen. We stayed until noon and then left for Nsawam, arriving around four thirty, just in time to be caught in a traffic jam in the town. We went to the market to buy yams, and then we were on our way to drop off Nana Afua at her place. On the way, we stopped by a nice restaurant, Royal Triangle, and had a couple of beers. It had a very nice ambience. Many people were gathered in an adjourning area, watching a soccer match.

When we arrived home, it was too late to tell Ama to prepare dinner, so Mrs. Rose, the tenant, made yams with tomato sauce; Osae's nephew brought us a can of corned beef hash. That was dinner.

MONDAY, MAY 10, 2010

We set off for Aburi to obtain some documents that Osae would need for his Ghanaian passport, as he was applying for dual citizenship. We had to see the Aburihene to get letters of reference. This process took some time because his assistant, although using word processing on a computer, made several errors that had to be corrected. When the papers were finally in order, it was too late to head for Accra. As we returned, we found the house of a young lady whom Osae had met at the ceremony, and he wanted to see her again. She prepared a meal for us. I washed my hands with local water, and I ate with my hands, African-style. Later, I became very ill, beginning with a bout of diarrhea that lasted most of the night. I took some of the medication I had and had a beer as we waited for Osae. We dropped off Nana Afua at her house and came home. Osae went back to see the young lady.

TUESDAY, MAY 11, 2010

We went back to Accra to work on getting Osae's documents together. I mailed my letters at the main post office. It was a real run-around, trying to find the right office to begin the process of reapplying for Ghanaian citizenship. Osae decided that he would deal with the process once he was back in the States. As we were returning, we stopped at the young lady's house for lunch/dinner, which consisted of plantains, fish, and meat stew. There was beer before the meal. We came in, and I spent the evening doing a crossword puzzle. Osae went back out.

THURSDAY, MAY 13, 2010

Osae received a call in the early morning, saying that the Queen Mother, the matron of the village, was having surgery on her hip and that she needed money for the copay. We left shortly afterward and picked up his nephew. We took the tortuous road to Aburi, found the hospital, gave the money, and then headed back. I was still excited about being able to play golf, since one of Osae's friend had previously invited me to play a round with him. The gentleman, however, called to say he was recuperating from an injury and was unable to play, but he would invite us to his house later. We went to Mary's house and had porridge and bread for a late breakfast; then we returned to the house. We stayed in the remainder of the afternoon, drank beer, and waited for dinner—yams with tilapia in a sauce. After dinner, I helped Joycelyn, the daughter of the woman who rented part of the house, who was a student at the university, with some review in psychology. She was studying a chapter on Sigmund Freud. I enjoyed it, professor that I am. Later, I did more puzzles and then went to bed.

FRIDAY, MAY 14, 2010

Osae had to visit villages. I woke up, got dressed, and waited for him. Since the wait was so long, I came back inside. As I was using the bathroom, Osae and his nephew left.

I found the charger to the battery for my camera, so I was able to charge it. I considered going to Accra because I hadn't heard from Osae. (As it turned out, he called me, but my phone was off.) When I called him, he said he'd taken the car to be serviced; a tire needed to be changed. He said that they would be back shortly, and we would have breakfast before starting out for the villages. Breakfast was *kinkey* and fried fish. Kinkey is mashed corn served with brown corn husks. It was a rather heavy breakfast, but it was around ten thirty before we started.

After breakfast, we went to the first village, where we were greeted with formalities. The secretary of the clan, Edu Agima, whom we picked up along the way, made the major presentations for us. I was asked to speak about what I wanted to do for the clan. We took some group pictures and then headed for the next village. There, we went through similar formalities, including pouring libations and drinking gin from the same glass. There were other speeches, and afterward we went to the shrine, a small locked room, where the ancestral stools, male and female, are kept. There was quite an elaborate ceremony that included pouring libations (schnapps) on the stools and chanting. We then took a small drink from the ancestral cup.

One of the issues raised during the formal ceremony was the unfinished school, so we went to visit it. The building was constructed— one room—but more windows were needed. Also, grass had grown almost waist-high from the floor of the building. It seemed feasible to accomplish this project. We later went to an elder's house and drank palm wine. Then we were on our way home, after dropping off the secretary and Nana Afua. We waited for dinner, even though it was only around five o'clock. Dinner came, rice and beef in a sauce. Things were quiet that evening as I waited for some time to pass so that I could place a call to Georgia and wish Blessid, my granddaughter, a happy eighth birthday. This was a profound and interesting day.

SATURDAY, MAY 15, 2010

I took my morning walk and lost ten cedis during the process. I had taken my phone with me, and as I looked at it to check the time, the cedis must have fallen from my pocket. After my walk, we had a breakfast of the leftover rice and beef stew, along with oranges and pineapples. Later, we decided to go to Accra to the Cultural Arts Markets, and we picked up Nana Dede so that she could assist us in bargaining for our items. I bought a few articles, but we were pressed for time. When we first arrived, we stopped at a shop next to the market and had a beer. Then we shopped for a while. Afterward, we met at the local restaurant and had lunch—rice and okra stew, with fish for me, along with a beer, which I was unable to finish. The food was good, but it gave me the runs later that evening. When we completed the shopping, we drove to Osae's relatives, a cousin and her husband. They were very nice. We were offered another beer. Then we drove back to Nsawan after dropping Nana Dede off at her place. I went to bed still suffering with diarrhea. What a night!

SUNDAY, MAY 16, 2010

As I was waking up, all I could hear was, "Baa, baa, baa." It sounded almost like a baby; actually, it was a baby, a lamb, all tied up, that had been brought for the meal for the day, a festive celebration. I got up to see what was going on. The lamb was bound by the legs and tied by the neck with a rope. It tried to get away as a fire was being started from the cooking area outside. As the fire continued to burn, the lamb was killed, with a cut through the jugular vein in the neck, the head partially severed. After the bleeding somewhat stopped, the whole lamb was placed over the fire and the hair was burned and shaved off with a knife. Then the entire lamb was exposed to the fire for a while. It was gutted and all the internal organs, which were in a sack, were removed. The meat was cut into smaller pieces, and the internal organs were exposed. The intestines were cleaned, and one could see the long string of feces. After all the meat was cleansed, it was seasoned and boiled for a while. Then it was cooled so that the seasoning could marinate. In the meantime, fufu was prepared, made from pounding cassava, then pounding plantains, separately. Finally, the two were mixed by additional pounding. At this time, I was asked to go inside and rest. I must have looked sleepy or sick from observing the action, but I didn't feel that way. Nevertheless, I did go inside and napped for almost two hours. When I awoke, more guests had arrived. My meal was presented to me, fufu and the lamb meat in a soup. Fufu is eaten with the fingers by taking pieces of what appears to be kneaded dough, ready to be baked, dipping it in the soup for flavor, and then swallowing it. The meat in the soup is taken and chewed. It was good, but the fufu was cold and the soup was hot. I enjoyed it but probably would have eaten more if the fufu had been warmer; it had been prepared while I slept. After eating, I changed my clothes and went outside to socialize with the guests. They were primarily Osae's family and friends. This was an enjoyable afternoon with food and drinks. When all the guests had left, I was happy to relax and prepare for bed. I called Calvin, my son in New York, to verify that he knew the itinerary for our return. Then it was a bath and off to bed.

MONDAY, MAY 17, 2010

Osae and I went for a long walk and talked about the US economy and his investments in Texas. We saw a young lady I had seen several times as I took my morning walks. She was friendly and walked with us to the house; we subsequently exchanged phone numbers. I wondered if she would walk with us on the remaining mornings. We came in and had breakfast. I hoped I'd get a chance to play golf in the afternoon, as Osae's friend said he would come for us around two o'clock. However, a major rainstorm occurred at eleven thirty. Plantain and palm trees were uprooted. As a result of this downpour, golf was no longer on the agenda. We decided to go to Accra and do more shopping at the market. After picking up Nana Dede on the way, we arrived about two hours later, since the rain and resulting mud slowed us down even more on the treacherous roads. I bought more things, always thinking I was getting a good price, but in reality, I paid through my ears and nose. However, I was satisfied with the items purchased. We had a beer and then headed back. Nana Dede agreed to cook dinner for us, so we went to her place and had yams and fish stew. Afterward, we returned home. I went to bed around eleven thirty so that I could get up early enough for my morning walk before we went to visit additional villages.

TUESDAY, MAY 18, 2010

While taking my morning walk, I encountered Edu Agima, the secretary of the clan, who would be accompanying us on the visits. He introduced me to his sister and said that he would come to the house at eight o'clock. When he arrived, we went to Kwesi's house because he had invited us for breakfast. We had a traditional *banku* (a corn and cassava dough dish) with fish soup. I ate it the Ghanaian way.

The first visit was a nine o'clock appointment at one of the chiefs' houses; he lived in the town of Nsawam, so he was close by. We went through the formalities and discussed the predicament of the clan. One major issue was the disenstoolment of a chief in the village of Aburi, not the aburihene, because there were eighteen charges against him. These charges had to be presented formally before the aburihene, and the accused would have the opportunity to address them. This was a lively discussion. The chief, who previously had a stroke but had recovered greatly, invited us to have a beer. I promised to give him some low-dose aspirin so that he could take them daily and hopefully avoid another stroke.

When we left, we headed for the nearby village to which I usually walked in the mornings. We didn't find the chief but were able to speak to his son, who gave us the father's cell phone number. When we came back to the house, I also gave Edu Agima some aspirin, and Osae gave him pain pills. When Edu Agima left, Osae and I went out and bought beer and Castle Bridge dry gin. We were expecting the company of the young lady I'd met during my walks, and she was bringing a friend.

When they arrived, we had an enjoyable time, talking and drinking.

After they left, Osae got dressed to go visit Nana Dede. I remained and waited for dinner. In the meantime, I took a nap to wear off some of the drinks—beer and gin. Dinner was excellent—plantains with fish and okra stew. I later declined an offer from the lady of the walks. It was difficult to sleep that night.

WEDNESDAY, MAY 19, 2010

I walked to the Ghana Commercial Bank to withdraw cedis from the ATM. The machine was not functioning, so I just walked back. I had breakfast; I'd requested some of last night's dinner—plantains with okra fish stew. After breakfast, I bathed and rested. Then I decided that I would take my shoes to have the inner sole glued back in place and return to the bank. I was successful this time, and on my way back, I found the shoemaker and had the work done. Later, as I was waiting for the gentleman to pick us up to play golf, I started to pack. Finally, the golfer's driver came to pick us up, but there was a misunderstanding on my part. The driver was taking us to the golfer's house for dinner and drinks, not to play golf. He had a very nice bungalow, which probably had belonged to a colonial dignitary in years past. We drank vodka with fruit juice and ate rice with fish stew. It was very good, but I couldn't eat a lot because I had a gaseous stomach. I really enjoyed the afternoon there. When we returned, many of Osae's family and friends came to wish us good-bye and safe journey. We exchanged final greetings and then went to bed very late, even though the golfer's driver was coming at four thirty in the morning with the Mercedes-Benz to take us to the airport.

THURSDAY, MAY 20, 2010

We left about five in the morning and took the back roads through Pokuase to avoid the traffic. We arrived at the airport very early, at six o'clock, but we did need the time to proceed through all the checkpoints and customs. I somehow got separated from Osae but was able to get through customs in time to have a breakfast sandwich and coffee. I even had a few minutes to shop at the duty-free shop, which had very few items and liquor but not much of a bargain. Most of the liquor I could purchase cheaper at a regular liquor store in New York.

We finally boarded the plane after the rain shower ended, though it was still drizzling a bit. The flight was fine and we arrived pretty much on time, even though we departed a half hour late. When we arrived, we had to wait on the tarmac for about forty-five minutes before we could taxi to the gate. Customs had long lines and too few agents. We finally got through and met Calvin, who drove us to Brooklyn—home, sweet home.

Thomas enjoying the sun in Tenerife, Canary Islands.

AFTERWORD

VALUE IN TRAVEL

The invaluable experiences of traveling abroad contribute to a knowledge base, both cognitive and affective, that enhances one's formal learning in traditional settings. If one is open-minded, willing to explore the unfamiliar, and receptive to differences (not ethnocentric or xenophobic), then visiting other countries and interacting with the people of those locales can be a priceless jewel that will be cherished forever. One must have the mind-set, that there is tremendous wisdom and knowledge that can be amassed, and this information may enrich one's life. I am happy to say that I have had myriad travels in my life.

In addition to my professional and academic trips, I have visited other locations, both domestic and international, on a more leisurely basis. It was a marvelous experience to see a live bull fight in Madrid and to walk through the Moors' construction of the Alhambra complex in Granada, all in Spain. For art historians, Florence, Italy, is equivalent to a trip to the Holy Land for Christians or a pilgrimage to Mecca for Muslims. It was amazing to see the works of Michelangelo, for example, the statue of David, and so many inspiring pieces in the various art galleries. The Canary Island of Tenerife, between Spain and Africa is a place of pleasure for Europeans, primarily, just as the Caribbean islands are for us North Americans. Even leisurely excursions can be a source of enlightenment if one expands the scope beyond the epicurean aspect of travel.

Highlights of my domestic travel include trips to Hawaii and Alaska. Hawaii is indeed paradise on earth. Reminiscing on the week spent in Maui, I can still envision the beautiful sunrises and sunsets glistening on the Pacific Ocean. While short vacations may not afford the opportunity to interact intimately with the local people—that is, learning their culture and experiencing their folklore—one can most certainly appreciate the physical environment that stimulates the sensory mechanisms within. In this relaxed state, one can physically, emotionally, and intellectually rejuvenate as one becomes more in tune with the beauty of the natural environment.

On a cruise to Alaska, what a wonderful experience there is in seeing glaciers from afar. What a revelation to learn that Alaska has summer weather—that is, temperatures in the eighties. Whale watching is also a popular activity while cruising the Alaskan waters.

I have had other traveling cruises, particularly to the Caribbean and surrounding area. Ports of call were Ocho Rios, Jamaica; Nassau, Bahamas; Cozumel, Mexico; Cartagena, Colombia; Limon, Costa Rica; and Colon, Panama. It is worth noting that the operation of the lock system as ships pass through the Panama Canal is a wonder in and of itself. I could go on and on about traveling, but I think I have made my point, and I am unapologetic. Yes, I am passionate about traveling and will always travel until I have made that final journey, where my soul will rest in tranquility.

Printed in the United States
By Bookmasters